I0005841

Asbury Theological Seminary

90th Anniversary

Publications

Audio Recordings from the 50th Anniversary Celebration
and Special Lecture Series
March 11-15, 1974

50th Anniversary Banquet Speeches
*by Franklin D. Morrison, Frank Bateman Stanger, and
J. C. McPheeters*

**"Salvation Today," "Ingredients of the Gospel,"
"The Mind of Christ," and "Keep the Hope of Heaven"**
by Bishop Roy C. Nichols

"Whither Wesleyan Theology?" in four parts
by Dr. Albert C. Outler

"Whiter Christology?" in four parts
by Dr. C.F.D. Moule

"Whither Mission?" in four parts
by Bishop Stephen Neill

The 90th Anniversary Publications are available in digital form for free through First Fruits Press. They can be found by visiting First Fruits' Website, under the Heritage Collection: place.asburyseminary.edu/firstfruits

The Distinctive Emphases

of

Asbury Theological Seminary

First Fruits Press
Wilmore, Kentucky
c2013

ISBN: 9781621711070

The Distinctive Emphases of Asbury Theological Seminary / Asbury Theological
Seminary. Fortieth Anniversary Committee ; Harold B. Kuhn, General Editor
First Fruits Press, © 2013 | Seminary Press, ©1963

Digital version at http://place.asburyseminary.edu/firstfruitsheritagematerial/29

First Fruits Press is a digital imprint of the Asbury Theological Seminary, B.L. Fisher Library.
Asbury Theological Seminary is the legal owner of the material previously published by the
Pentecostal Publishing Co. and reserves the right to release new editions of this material as
well as new material produced by Asbury Theological Seminary. Its publications are available
for noncommercial and educational uses, such as research, teaching and private study. First
Fruits Press has licensed the digital version of this work under the Creative Commons
Attribution Noncommercial 3.0 United States License. To view a copy of this license, visit
http://creativecommons.org/licenses/by-nc/3.0/us/.

For all other uses, contact:

First Fruits Press
B.L. Fisher Library
Asbury Theological Seminary
204 N. Lexington Ave.
Wilmore, KY 40390
http://place.asburyseminary.edu/firstfruits

Asbury Theological Seminary. Fortieth Anniversary Committee.
    The distinctive emphases of Asbury Theological Seminary / by the Asbury
    Theological Seminary. Fortieth Anniversary Committee ; Harold B. Kuhn, general
    editor.
    vi, 106 p. ; 21 cm.
    2nd ed. / revised by Faith E. Parry and Robert Danielson
    Wilmore, Ky. : First Fruits Press, c2013.
    Asbury Theological Seminary 90th Anniversary Publications ; no. 3
    Originally published: Wilmore, Ky. : Seminary Press, c1960.
    Includes bibliographical references.
    Contents: Introduction – The Wesleyan understanding of sin / Delbert R. Rose –
    The nature and extent of the atonement / William M. Arnett – The witness of the
    Spirit / Harold B. Kuhn – The doctrine of sanctification / George A. Turner.
    ISBN: 9781621711070 (pbk.)
    1. Theology, Doctrinal. 2. Methodist Church – Doctrines. 3. Asbury Theological
    Seminary. I. Title. II. Kuhn, Harold B. (Harold Barnes), 1911- III. Asbury Theological
    Seminary. IV. Series
    BT10 .A823 2013   230.08

Cover design by Kelli Dierdorf

asburyseminary.edu
800.2ASBURY
204 North Lexington Avenue
Wilmore, Kentucky 40390

First Fruits
THE ACADEMIC OPEN PRESS OF ASBURY SEMINARY

The Distinctive

Emphases

of

Asbury Theological

Seminary

Seminary Press
Wilmore, Kentucky
c1963

Preface

No observance of the anniversary of the founding of a graduate school of theology would be complete without significant publications. The Fortieth Anniversary Committee is pleased to present to the friends of Asbury Theological Seminary this significant trilogy of books: *Henry Clay Morrison Crusader Saint, The History of Asbury Theological Seminary,* and *The Distinctive Emphases of Asbury Theological Seminary.*

We congratulate the members of the Fortieth Anniversary Editorial Committee—Dr. Harold B. Kuhn, chairman, Dr. J. Harold Greenlee, and Dr. George A. Turner—for their excellent work, and we commend to you the careful reading of these three significant Fortieth Anniversary volumes.

Frank Bateman Stanger
President of the Seminary and
General Chairman of the Fortieth
Anniversary Committee

Table of Contents

Preface i

Introduction v

The Wesleyan Understanding of Sin 1
   Delbert R. Rose

The Nature and Extent of the Atonement 29
   William M. Arnett

The Witness of the Spirit 57
   Harold B. Kuhn

The Doctrine of Sanctification 81
   George A. Turner

Introduction

There is a body of central truths, which belong to the whole of Evangelical Christendom, which are held to be normative by all who maintain the historic Christian Faith. Within the Evangelical Christian position there are also legitimate differences of emphasis with respect to some of these things held in common. It has frequently been these differing emphases, which have enabled the several Christian denominations to enrich the Church's understanding of her total message.

Asbury Theological Seminary stands in the mid-stream of historic Christian Evangelicalism. It also maintains, as its distinctive message, a special emphasis upon the doctrinal principles that took shape in the eighteenth century in the Wesleyan movement. As an interdenominational, confessional institution, it believes that these Distinctives are worthy of sharing with the Church Ecumenical.

At the Fortieth Anniversary of Asbury Theological Seminary, it has been thought appropriate to issue this volume, setting forth, with what we hope may be a vivid freshness, four of the Seminary's doctrinal emphases. They are: the Wesleyan Doctrine of Sin, the Wesleyan understanding of the Atonement, the Wesleyan Doctrine of the Witness of the Spirit, and the Wesleyan Doctrine of Entire Sanctification. It is with the hope that these presentations may impress the reader with the contemporary relevance of these Wesleyan distinctives, and with the prayer that they may serve to build Christ's Church, that this volume is presented as part of an Anniversary Trilogy.

The Committee

The Wesleyan Understanding of Sin

Delbert R. Rose

Until very recent time few men even faintly dreamed of the vast reaches of Jesus' statement of nineteen centuries ago when He said, "But beware of men" (Matthew 10:17). As never before in human history "Man is not safe in the presence of man." Never before have the means for cheapening, brutalizing, and destroying human life been "so highly developed, so easy to use."[1]

With race suicide by nuclear and/or germ warfare a constant threat, how can man be brought to live at peace with himself when it appears that evil impulses are in the saddle and riding him toward his death? This is the problem of problems for those wrestling with the bases for human survival on this planet.

While all are ready to admit we face colossal problems, too many religionists as well as educators, scientists, and statesmen are still of the mind that "Our problems are man-made therefore they can be solved by man. And man can be as big as he wants. No problem of human destiny is beyond human beings."[2]

1

While granting that "our problems are man-made," no serious student of human nature, human history, and the Bible will concede that man is able to solve his basic problem. In spite of his "conversion" achievements in the realm of nature, man has been unable to remake himself; a change that it now appears will be absolutely necessary to human survival. Man's greatest unsolved problem is still man himself, and "the root of that problem is sin."[3] If the testimony of the centuries has any final significance, it witnesses incontrovertibly to the fact that man has always failed in the role of a "self-savior."

The Present Situation

Winds of political and theological optimism swept the western world during the closing decades of the nineteenth century and the opening decades of the twentieth. Western man, after centuries of strenuous effort to improve the face of nature and human society, felt he could relax under the balmy skies of an over-arching theological liberalism which expressed itself in two glowing, man-made "satellites": the inevitability of human progress and the essential goodness of man.

But World War I, the subsequent rise of Marxian Communism, Fascism, Nazism, and the outbreak of World War II with its concentration camps, gas chambers, human ovens, and Siberian exiles for the liquidating of millions of men, women, and children, sent mushrooming into the heavens the blackest clouds that had ever been seen on the human horizon. By the close of World War II the dream world of liberalism's making had become so darkened that one world-renowned sociologist declared the twentieth century thus far to be the most barbaric and inhumane of all the human centuries.

As far back as 1919, from a Swiss pastor's study, "contrary winds" of theology began to blow out across Europe and soon made themselves felt on our American shores. With the first edition of his commentary on Romans (*Der Roemerbrief*), Karl Barth showed how extremely shallow and irresponsibly complacent had been theological liberalism's interpretation of human nature. By the early 1930's American born Reinhold Niebuhr was launching devastating attacks upon liberal optimism and advocating a re-examination of "the biblical doctrine of original sin."

This was a timely preachment, for theological liberalism had about washed the idea of sin out of her thinking. The noted theologian William Adams Brown observed that one of the most prominent marks of religion in America during the 1920's was "a loss of the sense of sin." "You will hear ministers," he wrote, "preaching about almost everything else except the forgiveness of sins."[4]

Interestingly enough, Mary Frances Thelen in her book *Man As Sinner in Contemporary American Realistic Theology* points us to those professors of "the philosophy of religion and systematic theology in the major liberal seminaries during the first third of the twentieth century," and declares that they "have little in their writings on the subject of sin."[5] Were not these men the instructors of many of the ministers of whom Dr. Brown was speaking?

Since the mid-thirties, however, there has been a growing and vocal interest in the doctrine of man as sinner. It is around this doctrine that perhaps the basic divergences within Christendom take their rise. Such was the view of John C. Bennett in 1933 when he said, "I think that the best shortcut to an understanding of the present theological situation is to realize that liberalism diverges from orthodoxy and neo-orthodoxy in its various forms in its doctrine of man, and that other differences follow from that."[6]

Dr. Bennett might also have indicated that basic to those differences existing between orthodoxy and neo-orthodoxy is this self-same doctrine of man and his sin.

The Paradisiacal Sin

Many today believe that nineteenth-century science dealt a "death blow" to faith in Adam as the first man in the Garden of Eden and that Biblical scholarship must conform to the naturalistic conclusions of an evolutionary science. To such thinkers Adam and Eve can no longer be regarded as real persons, "the actual ancestors of the whole human race." Instead Adam is a symbol of humankind and its failure to choose and adjust properly in the ever-changing circumstances of life, which in turn necessitate ever-changing moral choices. Therefore the fall is not to be viewed as a sudden event in the past but as a continuing process in each person's life. It is to be conceived as that "tragic side of human experience" in which everyone finds himself when he rebels against God instead of living in the "blessedness of His service."[7] In this "reinterpretation of the Adam story" man's "original righteousness" is not something from which the first Adam fell, but the destiny for which we were divinely intended and toward which we should be moving.[8]

The Claims of Scripture

Varied as the interpretations of the Genesis record of man's creation and fall may have been or are now, historic Wesleyanism accepts the Biblical record of beginnings as the only trustworthy starting-point in understanding man. Instead of regarding "Adam as Every Man" or "Every Man as his own Adam," Wesleyanism understands Adam as a particular man, a person even as we are persons, as having had a history in this world of space, time, and matter even as we have our history within it. Instead of treating the fall as merely an allegory or "myth" with perennial historical relevance to us, Wesleyan scholars see these early chapters in Genesis as *an inspired record of historical facts, bound up with a deep and rich symbolism*,"[9] which is ever relevant for us.

The biblical bases for this position are these:

1) Chapters two and three of Genesis "purport to be genuine history" even as the other chapters do in this "book of beginnings" and are an integral part of the whole fifty chapters.
2) Until this present hour the Church generally, "with the exception of the dialectical theologians and their converts," has understood the Genesis record as intended to teach historical fact.
3) Not biblical exegesis but man's geological, biological, and psychological theories have produced this departure from a historical view of Genesis 1-3.
4) In both Old and New Testaments Adam is treated in a historically and genealogically meaningful sense (Genesis 5:1-5; 1 Chronicles 1:1; Luke 3:38; 1 Timothy 2:13-14; Jude 14).
5) The Apostle Paul builds, in a most basic way, his Christology upon the historical trustworthiness of the Genesis account of the first Adam, who was also the first man (Romans 5:12-20; 1 Corinthians 15:21-22, 45-49).

In these last Scriptures, Paul presents both Adam and Christ as historical persons in representative roles. To "demythologize" these Scriptures in the Bultmannian sense is to destroy all basis for treating the Bible in any of its parts in a grammatical and historical sense.[10]

The Capacity To Sin

The creation and fall of Adam must ever be viewed against the background of God's *relationship* to man and of man's *responsibility* to his Maker. "Only as we understand man in his vertical relationship, i.e., toward God, can we understand man in his horizontal relationships, i.e., toward the rest of the created universe."[11]

A varied, vital connection between God and man shines through the Biblical writings in place after place. God is his Creator (Genesis 1:26-28), Sustainer (Acts 17:25), Preserver (Psalms 145:15, 16; Matthew 5:45), Sovereign (King, Governor), Lawgiver, Judge, Savior (Isaiah 33:22; Acts 14: 15:17; James 4:12; Revelation 11:16-18; 19:1-8), and Heavenly Father (Luke 3:36-38; Acts 17:29).

When God said, "Let us make man in our image, after our likeness: and let them have dominion..." (Genesis 1:26, ARV), He was about to produce the noblest of all His moral creatures. As far as we know from the Scriptures, no other beings were specifically fashioned after the image and likeness of their Maker. It can rightly be said, "God is man's closest relative."

According to Wesley, man made in the image of God must be viewed in more than one dimension. First, man bore the stamp of the natural image of Deity, "a picture of His own immortality; a spiritual being, endued with understanding, freedom of will, and various affections." Inherent in this likeness to God was that which distinguished Adam and his descendants from all lesser creatures, namely their capacity to know, to love and to obey God.[12] The natural image may also be called "the essential image, which is summed up in the word personality."[13] This natural image of God in man gave him the capacity to bear God's political image, i.e., the ability to serve as the divinely ordained under-sovereign or ruler over this planet called Earth (Genesis 1:26-28).

However, it was not the natural or the political image in man, but God's moral image, which constituted the chief and most important likeness of Adam to God. According to Paul that moral image consisted of Adam's immediate, personal knowledge of God (Colossians 3:10) and his conformity to the "righteousness and true holiness" of Deity (Ephesians 4:24). Thus, man's original righteousness was "a power to do the good which he knew should be done, and which he inclined to do; even to fulfill the whole law of God. If it had not been so, God would not have required perfect obedience of him."[14]

In the beginning man's original righteousness was entire, diffused throughout his whole being; it was natural to his being, inclining him to love God with all his powers; it was mutable, that is, forfeitable, in danger of being lost. At his creation man's will was not left in a posture of neutrality or indifference to good and evil. "God set it towards good only, yet did not so fix it, that it could not alter; it was movable to evil, but by man himself only."[15] Inwardly and outwardly sinless, Adam had the power to remain that way as he continued in right relationship with God. But he also had the power, although not the right, to corrupt himself by choosing other than the divinely prescribed limits for his life.

The *capacity* to disobey, the power to choose contrary to the will of God, is not in itself sinful. Capacity as such is amoral. What a morally responsible being does with his powers of choice determines the moral quality of his actions and nature.

Placed in that Edenic environment, with all earthly creatures as his proper subjects and servants, Adam was to face the supreme moral test of his existence. Would he heed the command, "thou shalt not eat of it" (Genesis 2: 17), or would he yield to temptation and sin?

The Choice To Sin

With full knowledge of the divine law and the penalty attaching to its violation, our first parents listened to the lie of the Serpent, "ye shall not surely die" (Genesis 3:4), and doubted that God would fulfill His threatened punishment upon their disobedience. This unbelief generated pride and they soon thought themselves "wiser than God; capable of finding a better way to happiness than God had taught" them. Their pride gave birth to self-will, and soon they determined to do their own will instead of the will of their Heavenly Father. Self-will unleashed desires, which led to outward sinning: "She took thereof, and did eat; and she gave also unto her husband with her, and he did eat" (Genesis 3:6, ARV).

Adam's sin— an act of self-separation from God, deliberately performed— was not brought upon him by any necessity either from within or without. The Tempter was present to be sure, but the power to resist, as well as to yield to, that temptation was resident within him. Wesley rejected the view that the temptation to sin, which Adam felt so keenly, was in itself a sinful thing. [16] Neither could he believe that Adam had to have sinful tendencies in order to be seduced into disobedience. Adam followed legitimate desires beyond the bounds set by God for their proper satisfaction. Having refused God's will and rule over him, Adam became a rebel, choosing to be self-governed and to seek his pleasures and happiness in this world and in his own works. He thereby made I himself an *idolater*—"a lover of the world more than a lover of God."

The Consequences of Sin

While man could have chosen not to sin, he could not choose the effects caused by his sinning. Some of those effects issued directly from the wrong behavior of Adam, resulting in maladjustment to the processes of natural and moral law. Other effects were positively inflicted upon him by God as a judgment for his rebellion.

Death— spiritual, physical, and eternal- was the penalty God announced had already been affixed to broken law. Adam's disobedience produced within him an awareness of standing under judgment from God. Agitated by "guilt feelings" and a sense of moral unfitness for the presence of the Holy, our first parents fled from the gaze of Almighty God. The moment Adam tasted of the forbidden fruit, spiritual death took over in his soul, and satanic power enslaved him.

The fall resulted in the total loss of man's moral and spiritual likeness to God, but not in the loss of the capacity for God's likeness. Being deprived of the life and likeness of God within his spirit-nature, Adam forfeited the knowledge, righteousness, and true holiness in which he had been created (Ephesians 4:24; Colossians 3:10). In choosing to risk the breaking of God's commandment, Adam exchanged innocence for guilt, rest of soul for condemnation, holiness for uncleanness, happiness for sorrow, and peace with God for a tormenting fear of God, security for anxiety, and life for death.

While the *moral* image of God in man was destroyed by that first sin, the *natural* image of God in him was marred, placing man under handicaps and limitations which would never have been known apart from the fall. In his understanding, ignorance and mistakes displaced perfect human judgment. Conscience became defective; the powers of the soul for self-direction and self-discipline were weakened; and bodily appetites and desires were given an ascendancy, which has led men repeatedly to take on "the image of the beasts." [17]

The political image of God in man likewise suffered under that first disobedience. Whereas man was made to rule over the lower creation, he found himself threatened by an hostility arising within the animal kingdom and from a loss of mastery over his earthly environment.

The Curse Because of Sin

The earthly home as well as the essential humanity of Adam suffered severely under the fall. In the beginning, all nature as it came from the creative hand of God was good and functioned, at its various levels, in keeping with human wellbeing. With man as the principal channel of blessing between the Creator and the subhuman creation, it follows that man's relation to God would vitally affect the lesser orders of being and forms of creation. William R. Cannon sums up Wesley's view at this point:

> ...when man sinned and became by his own free act incapable of receiving, much less of transmitting, those divine blessings... the communication between God and the lower orders of creation was cut off; and the animals were denied those divine blessings which they had been created to receive. Thus every creature was subjected to pain and evil, not by the free choice of its own nature, but by man's sinful act, which God permitted and allowed so to effect his world.[18]

Wesley believed we could be "infallibly certain" that "there was no natural evil in the world, until it entered as a punishment of sin."[19]   Tracing the emphases of both Testaments, Wesley was convinced that had there been no sin, no moral evil, there would have been no suffering for man or beast in this world, no natural evils. He felt that tiresome and tedious labor, pain and anguish in childbearing, sickness and sorrow, disease and death- all bear witness to the curse resting upon mankind because of the fall.

The Pervasive Sinfulness

The paramount importance which Wesley gave to the doctrine of original sin is evidenced by its being the longest single treatise on any one subject found in his fourteen-volume set known as *The Works of John Wesley*. So basic is this doctrine to historic Wesleyanism that Wesley considered it "the very foundation of the whole plan of salvation, and made acceptance of it an essential mark of distinction between Christianity and heathenism."[20]

The Racial Connection

The first man stood as both the natural and the moral head of the human family, which he was physically endowed and divinely enjoined to procreate. Adam was the human father but also legal representative of the entire human race, which he carried potentially within him from the day of his creation. Unlike the angels which seem to have been singly and separately created by God, men were to have a racial connection, a biological tie, a lineal relationship, with a common father, which in turn constituted mankind, as a whole, a family of blood-brothers (Acts 17: 26).

Acting both as a private and a public person, Adam's behavior would bring measureless blessings or untold miseries upon his descendants. Under commission to beget children, who like himself would have both procreative and political powers, Adam was well aware that he could not live unto himself. He doubtless knew that his choices, rightly made, would have far-reaching effects for good upon all his offspring. But that a wrong choice would involve his posterity in penal consequences he seems not to have duly considered. With a racial connection between our first parents and the entire human family, Adam's choice and conduct could not but have powerful hereditary and environmental effects upon his descendants.

The Radical Corruption

Perhaps no less popular view of human nature could be championed in modem times than that of the hereditary corruption of mankind. To teach that we are "congenitally warped, deformed, diseased" in our moral and spiritual nature, is to propagate a "dreadfully damaging concept" of human nature, according to men like Dr. Brock Chisholm of the World Health Organization.[21] To the promoters of New England Unitarianism this belief in inherited sinfulness was a most "depressing account of human nature."[22] For them it was a denial of their faith in "the essential dignity and inherent worth of human nature in its entirety."[23]

But Willard L. Sperry has shown that when we listen closely to the "majority of biologists and anthropologists" and to the findings of depth-psychology, there is far more evidence to support the orthodox doctrine of original sin than there is the liberal view of man's *essential dignity*.[24]

Wesley himself was a close observer of his contemporaries, of men in history, and of the biblical teaching on the universality of sin. His missionary labors in Georgia caused him to revise his previously held theory of "the natural dignity of man and his noble desire to find God," and confirmed for him the Scripture's teaching that man is very far gone from original righteousness and that the imaginations of his heart are only evil continually (Genesis 6:5). So, whether considering the heathen world or the civilized world— including that part of it that has had the greatest Gospel benefits- Wesley saw sin as universally pervasive, as a radical corruption that has been handed down to us from Adam.[25]

While men may observe human nature and establish the fact of man's wickedness, only "special revelation" can give us the "how" and the "why" of human sinfulness.[26] What is the message then of special revelation on this matter? The Old Testament theologian, A. B. Davidson, summarizes the older Testament for us.

> The… conclusion to which the passages of the Old Testament lead us are these: *first*: that what is specifically called *original sin* is taught there very distinctly, i.e. 'that corruption of man's whole nature which is commonly called original sin,' that it is also taught that this sin is inherited; *second*, that no explanation is given in the Old Testament of the rationale of this inherited corruption beyond the assumption that the race is a unity, and each member of the race is sinful because the race is sinful.[27]

David's penitential prayer in Psalm 51 brings into sharp focus the fact of man's basic sinfulness at birth. "Wash me thoroughly from mine iniquity, and cleanse me from my sin… Behold, I was shapen in iniquity, and in sin did my mother conceive me" (Psalms 51:2, 5). This "sin" which the Psalmist is confessing and for which he is imploring deliverance, affirms A. B. Davidson, is inherited. Not he alone but all those around him are likewise sinful.[28] Some have interpreted this passage as teaching that the "act of conception, or procreation, is an act of sin," or that "the process of birth is impure."[29] Such a view would be utterly out of harmony with the original divine intention that man should procreate and populate the earth and subdue it (Genesis 1:28). What the Psalmist is acknowledging is that he and "his parents are part of the human race, and as such they carry the taint or stain of sin in the race."[30]

Turning to the New Testament we discover Paul is emphasizing the very same truths- the universality of sin and the pervasiveness of an inner sinfulness in man by virtue of his being a part of the human family.

> Wherefore, as by one man sin entered into the world, and death by sin, and so death passed upon all men, for that all have sinned...For...by one man's offence death reigned by one... Therefore, by the offence of one judgment came upon all men to condemnation...(Romans 5:12-18). ...among whom we also...were by nature children of wrath, even as the rest (Ephesians 2:3, ASV).

Paul's interpretation of our basic inner sinfulness is strongly supported by the words of Jesus Himself.

> That which cometh out of the man, that defileth the man. For from within, out of the heart of man, proceed evil thoughts, adulteries, fornications, murders, thefts, covetousness, wickedness, deceit, lasciviousness, an evil eye, blasphemy, pride, foolishness: All these evil things come from within, and defile the man (Mark 7:20-23).

In the New Testament a number of different terms are employed to designate this sinfulness in man's nature. It is referred to as the "sin" (Romans 6: 1-2, 11, 22; 7:8, 11, 14); "the flesh," used in the figurative sense, not the mortal body (Galatians 5: 19, 24; Romans 6: 12; 8: 11); "the carnal mind" or "the mind of the flesh" (Romans 8:6-7); "the body of this death" (Romans 7:24); occasionally "the old man" (Romans 6:6; Ephesians 4:22); "the body of sin" (Romans 6:6); "the law of sin" and "the law of sin and death" (Romans 7:23, 25; 8:2); and "the root of bitterness" (Hebrews 12:15). In no instance does the New Testament indicate that this original corruption is to be identified with our God-given humanity, either in the immaterial or in the material aspects of our composite nature. Sin is an alien factor, a force foreign to human nature, but one which nevertheless is operative in human beings from birth and as long as it is not dealt with by divine grace.

Some have claimed Wesley had a defective definition of sin because they assume his definition of "willful sin" is the extent to which he carried his concept. Few misunderstandings of Wesley could be farther from the truth about his basic views. To him sin was also an evil principle, which was inherited from Adam, and which needed the atoning merits as definitely as willful wrong. His sermons, "Sin in Believers" and "Repentance of Believers," cover this phase of man's problem rather thoroughly, and should serve as a corrective for those who think of Wesley's doctrine of sin as superficial, perhaps "Pelagian."

The Recurring Contamination

How is this basic sinfulness of human nature transmitted from generation to generation? Admittedly this is a perplexing matter. Wesley himself felt the mode of its transmission was as mysterious and unknown to us as the transmission of human nature both in its bodily and soulful aspects. He restricted himself to affirming the fact without constructing an explanation of it.[31]

Contemporary Wesleyan scholars, generally, favor some form of the "genetic transmission" theory because they see it as "simply an application of the law of heredity to man's total being."[32] Testing this principle biblically, one finds support for it in Genesis, where it declares that "God created man in his own image" (Genesis 1:27), but after the fall we read that "Adam...begat a son in his own likeness, after his image" (rather than in the image of God). Having forfeited his "original righteousness and holiness" Adam could not transmit a quality of holiness, which he no longer possessed.

The Required Correctives

Many have questioned the justice and goodness of God in allowing the sinfulness of Adam, with its attending miseries, to be transmitted to the entire human race. Wesley's response was this:

> The state of all mankind did so far depend on Adam, that, by his fall, they fell into sorrow, and pain, and death, spiritual and temporal. And all this is no ways inconsistent with either the justice or goodness of God, provided all may recover through the Second Adam, whatever they lost though the first; nay, and recover it with unspeakable gain; since every additional temptation they feel, by that corruption of their nature which is antecedent to their choice, will, if conquered by grace, be a means of adding to that 'exceeding and eternal weight of glory.'[33]

Rejecting the view that God *decreed* the fall of Adam (with its consequent miseries and depravity), Wesley and his adherents have always seen that the *permission* of sin (through Adam's responsible choice) is more than matched by the *provision* for every man's recovery through the last Adam, Jesus Christ. While God "so constituted the human race in the original act of creation that man's moral and spiritual nature, as well as his physical nature, should be transmitted from parent to child through all succeeding generations,"[34] yet no one this side of Adam will eventually be lost solely because of Adam's sin. Any and all who may be lost eternally will be those who have chosen to sin and to approve of the corruptions of "original sin" which they feel in their own natures. Let us consider Wesley's words at this point:

> This single consideration totally removes reflections on the divine justice or mercy, in making the state of all mankind so dependent on the behavior of their common parent; for not one child of man finally loses thereby, unless by his own choices; and every one who 'receives the grace of God in Christ,' will be an unspeakable gainer.[35]

Wesley believed in Adam's total fall and in human nature's total fall in Adam. But he did not believe that God left either Adam or the race in the total grip of sin. Instead, he taught that "prevenient grace" (that grace that *goes before* personal salvation) had been unconditionally bestowed (by virtue of Christ's atoning death) upon all mankind. This "prevenient grace" spared the race from extinction in Adam who deserved to die immediately for his crime; it clears all men from any and all guilt of Adam's actual sin, which might have been transmitted to his off-spring; it renders all men salvable by sustaining in man a capacity for God, for righteousness and true holiness; it enables man's natural powers to function so as to produce a tolerable state of affairs in human society; it also assists man in his response to the overtures of "saving grace" that he might be redeemed.

Therefore no human being has been left in "a state of mere nature," under the *unmitigated force* of sin's corruption, consequences, and curse. Instead, two principles are at work in him, fallen nature and divine *grace*, and these are contrary the one to the other. This easily accounts for the paradoxes confronting us in human nature. Wesley held these two truths together, as must we: the proneness to sin on man's part, and the drawing of man toward God and goodness on the Savior's part; for He is the light that lighteth every man coming into the world (John 1:9).[36]

Another word of caution and often correction is repeatedly needed when speaking of original sin— inherited depravity, transmitted corruption— in human nature. Not infrequently men have accused Wesley of implying that "inbred sin" is a substance, a thing, a material entity. Dr. George A. Turner has shown that the true Wesleyan position, from Wesley onward, has in reality avoided this pitfall. Sin does not inhere in man's body, the material aspect of his nature, but sin is a principal and dynamic force of, and for, evil within the immaterial aspect of man's nature, his spirit. While human language must be employed to designate and describe the workings of this inner evil reality, it must never be construed as being a substance.[37]

Some have likened "inbred sin" to a fever in the body, to a crookness in a gun-barrel, or to the electrical force in a magnetic field. In each analogy something immaterial, intangible, has been used to point to a condition, a factor, a force, which is not the same as, but just as real as, the material substance through which it manifests itself.

The Responsible Conduct

In his scholarly study on "John Wesley's Concept of Sin," Dr. Leo Cox has shown that Wesley viewed sin under three categories. First, sin as willful; second, sin as principle, third, sin as infirmity.[38] So distinct and separate are these phases of man's sin-problem that all three major areas of God's redemptive work *for* and *in* man are necessary to effect a full remedy for his total need. Sin as willful disobedience is dealt with in free justification. Sin as a polluting principle is dealt with in full sanctification. Sin as consequence, in the form of "infinities," is fully removed in final glorification.[39] Without carefully distinguishing the forms which sin takes in human nature and behavior we are left in moral confusion and/or self-contradictions when endeavoring rightly to handle the Word of truth concerning our salvation.

Wesley defined the *act of sin* as "a voluntary transgression of a known law."[40] Such acts are guilt-producing and death-dealing in their effects upon the soul. These give rise to what theologians call "acquired," as over against "inherited," depravity. Sins can be committed inwardly as well as outwardly by consenting to wrong attitudes. He who hates another is a murderer, according to New Testament standards (1 John 3:15); and he who "lusts" has already committed adultery in his heart (Matthew 5:28).

While it is generally recognized that men express their rebellious conduct through evil thoughts, words, and deeds, yet too few have distinguished between sins of "commission," "omission," "suspicion," "presumption," and "ignorance." These "categories" will help us see that sin has not always been treated in absolute terms in the Bible.

1) The "sins of commission" are violations of known commands to abstain from wrong-doing (1 John 3:4).

2) The "sins of omission" are violations of known duty to do the good that a person has the ability, knowledge and opportunity to perform (James 4:17).

3) The "sins of 'suspicion'" are those violations of conscience in either doing or neglecting something which cannot be done or omitted in "good faith" before God- these "break faith" with God by allowing "the questionable" to determine conduct, instead of known right and wrong. For "when we act apart from our faith we sin" (Romans 14:21-23, Philips).

4) The "sins of presumption" arise when we take for granted that God will do something for us which He has not promised, and therefore not obligated Himself, to do for men. Such a sin was suggested by Satan when tempting Jesus to leap down from the pinnacle of the Temple, urging Him to trust God to save Him from injury while deliberately violating the law of gravity (Matt. 4:5-7).

5) The "sins of ignorance" arise from doing or neglecting, unintentionally, that which is harmful to others and/or ourselves (Leviticus 4 and 5: Deuteronomy 19).

The "cities of refuge" in the Old Testament period were God's method of teaching His people the basic difference between intentional and unintentional wrong. The sacrificial offerings at the Tabernacle included those made for the "sins of ignorance," those wrongs committed unawares or that "attempted good" which fell short of the goal because of the lack of ability or wrong information. While we may pronounce the conduct of others good or bad, God alone knows the true motivation behind each man's thoughts, words, and deeds (1 Samuel 16: 7). Only He perceives the full guilt and depravity or the righteousness and true holiness of a soul before Him. It is motive behind each act that determines its moral quality before God.

> In the foregoing fivefold classification of sins it is apparent that as one moves from the first to the fifth categories, sins become increasingly subjective and personal- increasingly an individual relationship between the soul and God, conditioned upon each person's knowledge, conscience, and faith.[41]

While willful sins arise out of responsible action, and produce guilt and moral uncleanness in the soul, these are not to be identified with the inherited depravity, which prompted them. Individual men are not directly responsible for their inherited proneness to wrong, but they are responsible for yielding to its suggestions and pressures. They become responsible for this evil principle itself when they see its exceeding sinfulness and the remedy for it in Jesus Christ.

Wesleyans clearly distinguish between willful wrong, cared for by God's justifying grace, and inherited pollution, cared for in God's full sanctifying grace, and those remaining infirmities which are not cared for until the resurrection of the body in final glorification (Philippians 3:20, 21). These "infirmities" are not of the nature of sin in the sense that they are willed or that they are in essence evil. But they do produce those "sins of ignorance" which can be as harmful at times as if they had been evilly intended.

These "sins of ignorance" are not guilt-producing or soul-contaminating as long as the believer is trusting the meritorious work of Christ and walking in the spiritual light which God has given him. They are the consequences that flow from a scarred human personality through which man's immortal spirit is seeking to express itself.

Careful distinctions must be made between sin as corruption of man's moral nature, and the consequences of sin, which scar rational and bodily aspects of man's being. Diseases and the scars they leave upon the human body are carefully distinguished by medical science; likewise to be distinguished are sin's existence in the heart and its lingering effects even after the heart has been cleansed.[42]

In Wesleyan thought these distinctions are constantly made:

1) The sinner before his "new birth" (justification) has (a) sins, (b) inbred sin, and (c) infirmities.
2) The "born again" person still has (b) inbred sin ("sin remains but it does not reign") and (c) infirmities.
3) The entirely sanctified believer has (c) infirmities of body and mind; but
4) The resurrected saint will have been delivered from all infirmities, which have scarred his personality in this life.

Wesley claimed, "although every sin is a transgression of the law, it does not follow that every transgression of a law is sin."[43] When sin is so defined as to cover any and every lack of "conformity to the divine law or standard of excellence,"[44] it means man is constantly a sinner and ever standing under the condemnation of God. Wesley rejected this view because he found it both contradicted Scripture (such as Romans 5:1; 6:22,

8:1; 1 John 3:9; 2:6) and the inward testimony of the Holy Spirit to the obedient believer's heart (Romans 8: 16; 1 John 3:21, 24).

We must remember that Adam before the fall lived under the *Edenic law* of inner and outer conformity to the whole will of God. In his unfallen human nature—free from all the scarring limitations he later was to know—he was empowered to conform perfectly "to the divine law or standard of excellence." But since the fall God has not held the *Edenic* standard over men and demanded their attaining to it. Instead, Christians are called to live under the *Evangelical law of love*, which requires loving God with all the heart, soul, mind, and strength, and one's neighbor as himself. By means of God's love shed abroad in his heart by the Holy Spirit the believer is enabled to fulfill the requirements of the divine law for him in this life, inasmuch as "he that loveth another hath fulfilled the law...since love is the fulfilling of the law" (Romans 13:8, 10).

The margin between what a perfect Adam attained under the *Edenic law* and what a perfect-hearted Christian realizes under the Evangelical law is covered by the atoning merits of Christ. God does not impute to believers as sin those "shortcomings" which arise out of a defective body and mind, yet they need the atoning merits of Christ in the light of God's perfect law, His absolute righteousness. Paul doubtless had all this in mind when he wrote, "...for where no law is, there is no transgression" (Romans 4: 15), and "...sin is not imputed when there is no law" (5: 13).

Christians are not called to live under past *Edenic law* nor are they now held to the standard of *Eternity's* law of the future. The present gospel dispensation operates under the *Evangelical law of love*. God holds us responsible now for loving Him with all our heart, soul, mind, and strength, and our neighbors, as ourselves; He does not require of us a *faultless conformity* to what an unfallen Adam attained or to what all the redeemed in heaven will perpetually achieve.[45]

The heart made perfect in love is compatible with a thousand infirmities, but not compatible with one willful sin, or with the sin principle we inherited from Adam (2 Corinthians 12:9-10; Romans 6: 1-2, 15-16; 1 John 2:5).[46]

In summary, the human predicament in this crucial hour, as in every era of history, is rooted in the paradisiacal sin of Adam and in the pervasive sinfulness of the entire human race, which stems from ancient Eden. But Evangelical Christianity, as it has expressed itself in and through the Wesleyan wing of the Church, proclaims a perfect Savior— One who is able to save us here and now from our willful sinning with its penalties and acquired depravities, and from our inherited sin with its power and pollution. Then in the blessed Hereafter He will permanently release us from all of sin's scars, derived from original sin and/or our own sinning.

Notes

[1] Norman Cousins, *In Place of Folly*. New York: Washington Square Press, Inc., 1962. pp. 4, 170.

[2] Quoted by Bruce Biossat, "Kennedy Foresees Peace on Gradual Evolution," *The Lexington Leader*. Lexington, Kentucky. June 18, 1963. p. 4.

[3] H. F. Rall, "From Harris Franklin Rall," *Religion in Life*, XXI (Spring, 1952), 187.

[4] William Adams Brown, *Beliefs That Matter*. New York: Charles Scribner's Sons, 1928. p. 126.

[5] Mary Francis Thelen, *Man As Sinner in Contemporary American Realistic Theology*. Morningside Heights, N. Y.: King's Crown Press, 1946. p. 13.

[6] John C. Bennett, "After Liberalism—What?" *The Christian Century*, L (Nov. 8, 1933), 1403.

[7] John Lawson, *Selections from John Wesley's 'Notes on the New Testament.'* Chicago: Alec R. Allenson, 1955. p. 77.

[8] Colin W. Williams, *John Wesley's Theology Today.* Nashville: Abingdon Press, 1960. p. 56.

[9] H. Orton Wiley, *Christian Theology.* Kansas City, Mo.: Beacon Hill Press, 1947. II, 52. (*Italics* added).

[10] John H. Gerstner, "The Origin and Nature of Man: Imago Dei," in *Basic Christian Doctrines*, Carl F. H. Henry, editor. New York: Holt, Rinehart and Winston, 1962. p. 91.

[11] Addison H. Leitch, *Interpreting Basic Theology*. Great Neck, N. Y.: Channel Press, Inc., 1961. p. 48.

---

[12] John Wesley, "The General Deliverance," *Sermons on Several Occasions.* New York: Phillips & Hunt, n.d. II, 50 ff. (Hereafter referred to as *Sermons*).

[13] William M. Arnett, "The Wesleyan Arminian Teaching on Sin," *Insights Into Holiness*, Kenneth Geiger, ed. Kansas City, Mo.: Beacon Hill Press, 1962. p. 58.

[14] John Wesley, *The Works of John Wesley.* Grand Rapids: Zondervan Publishing House, n.d. IX, 435. (Hereafter referred to as *Works*).

[15] *Ibid.,* 436.

[16] *Sermons*, II, 70.

[17] *Works,* VI, 216-223.

[18] William R. Cannon, *The Theology of John Wesley.* Nashville, Abingdon-Cokesbury Press, 1946. p. 197.

[19] *Works*, IX, 321.

[20] Leo G. Cox, "John Wesley's Concept of Sin," An Unpublished Master of Arts Thesis in the School of Religion in the Graduate College of the State University of Iowa. February 1957. p. 4.

[21] Edith Hunter, "Neo-Orthodoxy Goes to Kindergarten," *Religion in Life*, XX (Winter 1950-1951), 9.

[22] Willard L. Sperry, "Sin and Salvation," *ibid.*, XXI (Spring 1952), 165.

[23] *Ibid.*

[24] *Ibid.,* pp. 168-69.

[25] *Works,* VI. 253-267.

[26] *Works,* IX, 239.

[27] A. B. Davidson, *The Theology of the Old Testament*. New York: Charles Scribner's Sons, 1904. p. 225.

[28] *Ibid.*, pp. 232-33.

[29] W. T. Purkiser, ed., *Exploring Our Christian Faith*. Kansas City, Mo.: Beacon Hill Press, 1962. p. 239.

[30] *Ibid.*

[31] *Works,* IX, 335-36.

[32] Purkiser, *op. cit.,* p. 239.

[33] *Works,* IX, 332.

[34] Cannon, *op. cit.,* 199.

[35] *Works,* IX, 332.

[36] Cox, *op. cit.,* 110-116.

[37] George A. Turner, *The More Excellent Way*. Winona Lake, Indiana: Light and Life Press, 1952. pp. 247ff.

[38] Cox, *op. cit.,* 110-160.

[39] *Ibid.*

[40] *Works,* VI, 417.

[41] Unpublished Statement on "The Doctrine of Sin" by the National Holiness Association, Dayton, Ohio, April 16, 1955. Delbert R. Rose, Reporter.

[42] *Ibid.*

[43] *Works,* VI, 417.

[44] Charles Hodge, *Systematic Theology.* New York: Charles Scribner's Sons, 1893. II, 186-87.

[45] *Works.* VI, 411-24.

[46] *Ibid.*

The Nature and Extent of the Atonement

William M. Arnett

The Cross of Christ is the heart of Christianity. The primary theme of the Bible is redemption, and the vital center of the redemptive activity of God is the death of Christ. The Cross is crucial not only for the Gospel story, but for history itself. The astounding fact of Holy Scripture is a crucified yet triumphant Savior.

Calvary's Cross is the focal point of diverse yet interrelated factors, which are exceedingly vital to the Christian faith, while from that center there radiates vast implications that stagger the human mind. Its dimensions are such that it speaks of both simplicity and profundity. Dr. James Denney reminds us that "the simplest truth of the gospel and the profoundest truth of theology must be put in the same words— He bore our sin."[1] The Cross represents Divine initiative in solving man's dilemma, for God "was in Christ reconciling the world unto Himself" (2 Corinthians 5: 19). It tells us in grim though eloquent language that redemption is costly yet glorious business, for it speaks of sacrifice that reaches up to the very nature and heart of God Himself. Indeed, "there was a cross in the heart of God before there was one planted on the green hill outside Jerusalem"[2] for Christ was "the lamb slain from the foundation of the world" (Revelation 13:8b).

God's atoning deed in Christ has implications of deep significance. It serves always to remind us that a moral structure underlies our universe, and that there can be no compromise or appeasement between goodness and evil. The climactic battle between Holy Love and the powers of evil was fought at the arena of Calvary's Cross, and Holy Love conquered by suffering to the uttermost of the Cross tells us that love, not evil, is the final power in the universe. The vast reach of the Cross is also significant, for it is both personal and cosmic. It was by the grace of God that Jesus "should taste death for every man" (Hebrews 2:9). Hence no man can dissociate himself from the scandal of the Cross. The enormity of my sin can be known only when I face the fact of the Cross. It is there that I become fully aware that sin is not a surface blemish, but a radical evil in the human heart. There is cosmical significance in "the blood of His cross" whereby there will be the ultimate resolution of all discords in the universe at large (cf. Colossians 1:20). The Cross suggests also the futility of man's schemes and panaceas to solve his basic problems apart from Divine grace. A final implication of the Cross is in regard to suffering. The Sinless One Who "suffered under Pontius Pilate" has enabled multitudes to bear their pain patiently and triumphantly, knowing that He "hath borne our griefs, and carried our sorrows" (Isaiah 53:4). While knowing that suffering is a terrible reality and recognizing that it involves elements of mystery, Christianity takes its stand at the Cross, which suggests the positive and constructive uses of suffering.

These introductory observations indicate some of the various facets of the atonement. The following discussion seeks to focus attention on some of the significant phases of the subject, including its meaning, its importance, its biblical necessity, its nature, and its extent and benefits. Brief consideration is also given to representative theories, which have been propounded concerning the atonement.

The Meaning of the Atonement

The basic meaning of the Christian doctrine of atonement is that "Christ died for our sins according to the scriptures" (1 Corinthians 15:3). Briefly stated, the atonement is the work of God in Christ for man's salvation.[3] Viewed in a larger perspective, a more elaborate definition would be necessary,[4] but the heart of the matter is stated in these few words.

Three basic factors are involved in a true meaning of the atonement: (1) The Love of God; (2) The Sin of Man; (3) The Plan of Substitution.

The Love of God

Calvary's Cross has its origin in the loving heart of God. The Golden Text of the whole Bible is that "God so loved the world, that he gave his only begotten Son, that whosoever believeth in him should not perish, but have everlasting life" (John 3:16).[5] As H. Orton Wiley observed, "the atonement, whether in its motive, its purpose, or its extent must be understood as the provision and expression of God's righteous and holy love."[6] Paul wrote that "God commendeth his love toward us, in that, while we were yet sinners, Christ died for us" (Romans 5:8). The Apostle's testimony is: "The Son of God ...loved me, and gave himself for me" (Galatians 2:20). Christ's life and death are the expression of God's love for sinful men, not the producing cause of that love. There is no conflict between the Father and the Son in the work of redemption.

The love of Calvary is the love of God. The love of Christ is the love of God. Paul calls it "the love of God which is in Christ Jesus our Lord" (Romans 8:39). The Cross is God's sufficient answer of love to a supreme need.

The Sin of Man

It is a basic assertion of Christian theology that man, on account of his sinful and rebellious nature, which is further manifest in willful disobedience and sin, is out of his normal relations with God, and cannot by deeds of his own rectify that situation (Cf. Romans 3:9, 10, 19, 20; 5:6, 8, 10). The result is that man is lost, alienated from God, a needy creature in a far country. He is sinful and he is a sinner. At the same time, there is a restiveness on man's part, due largely to God's prevenient grace, whereby he longs for fellowship with God. Very often, however, his search is badly perverted, even expressing itself in hostility to his Creator, the source of man's true being.

It is the witness of the New Testament that Christ's death is closely connected with man's sin. It speaks of His blood as shed "for the remission of sins" (Matthew 26:28). It tells us that "Christ also hath once suffered for sins, the just for the unjust, that he might bring us to God" (1 Peter 3:18).

The Plan of Substitution

One of the most important aspects in understanding the meaning of the atonement from an evangelical point of view is that Christ's death is vicarious or substitutionary. He came "to give his life a ransom for many" (Mark 15:34). In explaining the purpose of His death He said, "I lay down my life for the sheep" (John 10:15). Jesus offered Himself as a sacrifice in our stead, bearing our sin in His own body on Calvary's Cross (Cf. 1 Peter 2:24). In order to put away sin He must take it upon Himself, and be "made sin for us" (2 Corinthians 5:21). His identification with sinners in His death also underlies these words: "Christ hath redeemed us from the curse of the law, being made a curse for us" (Galatians 3:13). This can only mean that Christ bore the curse that sinners should have borne. He was our substitute. In His death He suffered not only the awful physical anguish, but also the tremendous spiritual horror of becoming identified with the sin to which He was infinitely opposed.

> Bearing shame and scoffing rude, In my place condemned He stood; Sealed my pardon with His blood: Hallelujah! What a Savior!

Such holy, selfless activity is amazing grace! One of the tragedies of modern theology is a tendency to reject the concept of substitution.[7] This, of course, amounts to a denial of biblical authority, because the idea of substitution is to be found in many places in the Scriptures.[8] It is a biblical truth that can be inadequately presented or easily caricatured, but it cannot be eliminated in an objective approach to the Bible. Only two alternatives are possible: Either Jesus Christ bore the burden of our sin, or we bear it. Christianity ceases to be a *redemptive* religion, and the Gospel loses its intelligibility and power, if we deny the truth that Jesus Christ took our place as sinners, and that in that place he did something for our salvation, which we could not do for ourselves.

The Importance of the Atonement

The Atonement of Christ is inseparable from other aspects of His career, including the Incarnation, the Ministry, the Resurrection, and the Ascension.[9] There is an organic wholeness concerning the work of our Lord, and therefore one phase should not be stressed in complete isolation from the rest. Calvary's Cross, however, is the heart of Christ's career, as we have already observed. The atonement "shifts the center of gravity in the New Testament," and by so doing "not Bethlehem, but Calvary, is the focus of revelation," as Denney has so forcibly pointed out.[10] The supreme importance of Christ's death is evident for several reasons.

It is a Prophetic Theme in the Old Testament

The foreshadowing of the atonement is conspicuous in the various types and prophecies throughout the Old Testament. The "scarlet cord" begins with the "Protevangelium" in Genesis 3:15 with the promise that the seed of the woman would bruise the serpent's head. Conspicuous among the types or symbols are: the blood sacrifice of Abel (Genesis 4:4); the ram on Mount Moriah (Genesis 22:13); the Passover lamb in Egypt (Exodus 12:1-28); the Levitical sacrifices (Leviticus 1-7); the offerings of Samuel (1 Samuel 7:9, 10); David (2 Samuel 6:18); Elijah (1 Kings 18:38); and Hezekiah (2 Chronicles 29:21-24). These random selections point unmistakably to the great offering to be made once for all by God's Son. The core and climax of Old Testament prophecy is the fifty-third chapter of Isaiah where a four-fold emphasis is discernible concerning the Suffering Servant of Jehovah.[11]

He was:

1) A *Victim* (vs. 4 "smitten of God, and afflicted"; vs. 10 "it pleased the Lord to bruise him; he hath put him to grief")
2) A *Voluntary Victim* (vs. 7 "he is brought as a lamb to the slaughter, and as a sheep before her shearers is dumb, so he openth not his mouth")
3) A *Vicarious Victim* (vs. 5 "He was wounded for our transgressions, He was bruised for our iniquities"; cf. vss. 6, 10, 11, 12 also
4) A *Victorious Victim* (vs. 10 "The pleasure of the Lord shall prosper in his hand"; cf. vs. 11 also).

It is a Prominent Theme in the New Testament

The importance of Christ's death can be noted in the fact that the earliest life of Jesus, the Gospel according to Mark, devotes nearly one-half of its messages to the death of Christ. In fact, the narrative of Christ's life in the four Gospels gives about one-fifth of the account to the passion of our Lord in the last three days of His earthly life. It has been pointed out that one out of every forty-four verses in the New Testament deals with this theme,[12] and R. A. Torrey observed that the death of Christ is mentioned directly more than 175 times in the New Testament.[13]

It is the Primary Purpose of the Incarnation

The Incarnation and Atonement are inextricably bound together in the redemptive work of Christ. In the relatedness of these two great Christological facts, we must agree with Dr. H. Orton Wiley that "the primary purpose of our Lord's assumption of 'flesh and blood' was to provide atonement by sacrificial death."[14] "He was manifested to take away our sins" (1 John 3:5). Jesus Christ came into this world to give His life a ransom for many (Matthew 20:28). He partook of flesh and blood in order that He might die (Hebrews 2:14). Thus the Incarnation is a pledge and anticipation of the work of Atonement. Christ did not come primarily to set us an example, or to teach a code of ethics. He came to die for us.

It is the Central Theme of the Gospel

In the Apostle's presentation of the marrow of the Gospel, he declared "first of all" that "Christ died for our sins" (1 Corinthians 15:3). The Ten Commandments, the Sermon on the Mount, and the teaching and example of Christ have their place in the proclamation of the Gospel in that they constrain us to realize our sin, and therefore our need of a Savior. However these phases of biblical teaching do not provide the remedy for sin but point forward to the death of Christ as the only possible solution.

It is Fundamental to Christianity

The uniqueness of Christianity is in the fact that it is distinctly a religion of atonement. The redemptive feature of the Christian faith distinguishes it from any and all other religions. Ethnic religions base their claim to authoritativeness on the teachings of their founders. While laying stress on the teachings of Christ, the uniqueness of Christianity is in the significance it assigns to the death and resurrection of its founder as the Divine Son of God. Remove the Cross of Christ from the Christian Gospel and its redemptive message is gone. Christ "loved me, and gave himself for me" (Galatians 2:20) is not only the testimony of Paul, but also the testimony of every Christian.

It is Essential to Man's Salvation

The language of the imperative, an urgent "must," is used repeatedly in regard to the death of Christ. If it is necessary for men to be *born again* in order to enter the kingdom of heaven, then the Son of Man must be lifted up if mankind is to be saved from perishing (cf. John 3:5, 7, 14, 15). If holiness is essential for men "to see the Lord" (Hebrews 12:14), then Jesus must suffer for His people beyond the gate at Jerusalem (Hebrews 13:12). If God is to remain just and yet be able to justify sinners, then the death of His Son is imperative (cf. Romans 3:25, 26). It is precisely for this season that Jesus repeatedly declared that He must suffer many things, be killed, and be raised up the third day (Matthew 16:21; Mark 8:31; Luke 9:22, 17:25; John 12:32-34; cf. Luke 24:46-48 also). If men are to be saved from sin, from the Divine standpoint the death of Christ is an absolute necessity.

It is the Grand Theme in Heaven

The focal point in the eternal city of the redeemed is "a Lamb as it had been slain." The Lamb is "in the midst" (Revelation 5:6). That Lamb is the object of praise in heaven, with both redeemed men and unfallen angels extolling the virtues of the One who made the salvation of lost men possible. The song of redemption is "destined to be sung through all eternity."[15] "Worthy is the Lamb that was slain to receive power, and riches, and wisdom, and strength, and honor, and glory, and blessing" (Revelations 5:12). How significant that of the more than one hundred names given to the Lord Jesus Christ in Scripture, the one that is to be perpetuated in heaven and throughout eternity is the "Lamb."

These considerations are sufficient to convince us that the doctrine of the Atonement lies at the very heart of the Gospel, which is the power of God unto salvation to everyone that believes.

The Necessity for the Atonement

The necessity for atonement is very closely related to the question of its nature. Therefore the discussion in this area will be limited to the basic factors involved, some of which will be given more elaborate consideration under the nature and results of the atonement.

There are three discernible strains in the Scripture, which are bound very closely together. These are: (1) the grim reality of sin; (2) God's willingness to forgive sin; and (3) the need of costly atonement. It is not difficult to trace these interrelated factors in the Bible. We have already noted man's sinfulness. Though highly created, he is deeply fallen. He is "dead in trespasses and sins" (Ephesians 2:1); his heart is "deceitful above all things and exceedingly corrupt" (Jeremiah 17:9 ASV). All men are "by nature the children of wrath, even as others" (Ephesians 2:3). The result of his sinful condition is three-fold: (1) alienation from God; (2) the wrath of God; and (3) bondage to sin and Satan. In his plight, man cannot save himself.

But the Scripture also declares that God, who is infinite, eternal, transcendent, dwelling in light unapproachable, whom no man has seen or can see, is willing, under favorable conditions, to pardon sin freely and abundantly (cf. Isaiah 55:7). But man, who was made to worship God, is a rebel, a transgressor of Divine law, and is at enmity against God. Since God is not only perfectly holy, but also the source and pattern of holiness, He should not and cannot deal lightly with sin. The necessities of His own being, the fact that He is the origin and upholder of the moral order of the universe, make it impossible for Him to compromise the claims of holiness. The Judge of all the earth *must* do right (cf. Genesis 18:25). He *must* be just. If sin is to be forgiven at all, it must be on some basis, which would not only vindicate His own being, but His holy law as well. Such vindication is supremely costly.

With these various factors involved, centering chiefly in God's holiness and man's sinfulness, the question naturally arises how God's love and mercy can be manifested so that His holiness will not be compromised by assuming a merciful attitude toward sinful men in the granting of forgiveness, pardon, justification. Who is to pay the infinite cost of Divine vindication? The answer to these questions bears witness to the supreme paradox of the Christian faith, that God Himself undertook to pay the cost, "to offer a sacrifice, so tremendous that the gravity of His condemnation of sin should be absolutely beyond question even as He forgave it, while at the same time the Love which impelled Him to pay the price would be the wonder of angels, and would call forth the worshipping gratitude of the redeemed. On Calvary this price was paid, paid by God: the Son giving Himself, bearing our sin and its curse; the Father giving the Son, His only Son Whom He loved. But it was paid by God become Man, Who not only took the place of guilty man, but also was his Representative."[16] This is the Lord's doing and it is marvelous in our eyes (cf. Psalm 118:23). The great Creator is Himself Redeemer.

The Nature of the Atonement

Various facets of the atonement must be considered if we are to understand its nature. The meaning of original biblical terms is an indispensable phase. The Bible, which is always the authoritative source for our Christian faith, repeatedly focuses attention on "the blood," and the meaning of this term must necessarily be explored. We have just noted that Godward and manward factors are involved. Therefore, in this section consideration is given to: (1) Biblical Concepts and Terminology; (2) The Meaning of the Blood; (3) The Godward Aspects; and (4) The Manward Aspects.

(1) Biblical Concepts and Terminology (a) The Old Testament (i) *Sacrifice*

The Old Testament presents the history of sacrificial worship from the very primitive period until it was fulfilled and abrogated by the atoning work of Christ who as "our Passover is sacrificed for us" (1 Corinthians 5:7b). The blood sacrifices of Abel (Genesis 4:3, 4), Noah (Genesis 8:20, 21) and Abraham (Genesis 15:9-21) conveyed a two-fold emphasis: 1) the necessity of dependence upon God, and 2) the sacrificial altar as an essential element in the approach to Deity. Furthermore, these sacrifices were expiatory in character, for there was a stern prohibition against the use of blood as food. "But the flesh with the life thereof, which is the blood thereof, shall ye not eat" (Genesis 9:4). Abel's blood offering was pleasing to God, resulting in Divine pardon and acceptance, for by it he "obtained witness that he was righteous" (Hebrews 11:4).

The Sacrifices of the Law under the Mosaic economy which further advanced and elaborated the sacrificial system (e.g., The Book of Leviticus), were later supplemented by the predictions of the prophets concerning the sacrificial sufferings and death of the Messiah, reaching their peak in Isaiah 53.

(1) Biblical Concepts and Terminology (a) The Old Testament (ii) *Kaphar*

The Hebrew word *kaphar*, a verb form that occurs over one hundred times in the Old Testament, is significant. It means literally "to cover." Noah, for example, was instructed to "pitch" (*kaphar*) the ark, that is, to cover it with pitch, suggesting protection from the waters of judgment. The cognate forms of this word *kaphar* are used in a similar sense to New Testament words meaning "atonement" as in Exodus 30:10, 15; Leviticus 1:4; 16:17, 30, 34. Thus, by the blood of animal sacrifices, the covering of human sin was provided (cf. Leviticus 16), anticipating, of course, the precious blood of Christ "as of a lamb without blemish and without spot" (1 Peter 1:19).

(1) Biblical Concepts and Terminology (b) The New Testament (i) Propitiation

In *Webster's New Collegiate Dictionary*, "to propitiate" is defined as "to appease and render favorable." We have already seen that man's sinfulness results in his estrangement from God and his exposure to the wrath of God. The thought of

God's wrath against sin and sinners is very prevalent in Scripture. In the Old Testament the more than twenty words, which are used to express the wrath of God, occur over 580 times.[17] This theme occurs less frequently in the New Testament, but when it does appear it is even more emphatic than in the Old Testament (e.g. John 3:36; Romans 1:18; 2:5; Ephesians 5:6; 1 Thessalonians 1:10; Hebrews 3:11; Revelations 19:15). However, God Himself in His infinite mercy and love has provided a means whereby Divine wrath against sinners could be averted. Thus "...God sent his Son to be the propitiation for our sins" (1 John 4:10). Paul says that God set forth His Son as a "propitiatory" sacrifice (Romans 3:25). God's holy wrath against sin is appeased by the death of Christ. However, the Christian idea of propitiation should not be conceived as a turning of God's wrath into love, but as "the provision of his love in order that his wrath may be averted in full consistency with his moral nature."[18]

Commenting on the equivalent Greek word for propitiation, *hilasmos* (which appears with its cognates approximately eight times in the New Testament and as often as 221 times in the Septuagint), and a closely related term, *katallage* ("reconciliation"), William Burt Pope made these very important observations: "Both these verbs have God for the subject and not for the object. The Supreme Being reconciles the world to Himself; it is not said that He is reconciled: this simply gives expression to the great truth that the whole provision for the re-establishment of peace is from above. God is reconciled to man, but *in Christ* who is Himself God: He therefore is the Reconciler while He is the Reconciled. So also the word expiate refers to an act of God: it is not said that He is propitiated, but that He propitiates Himself or brings Himself near by providing an expiation for the sin. Strictly speaking the atoning sacrifice declares a propitiation already in the Divine heart."[19] These important thoughts and distinctions need to be pondered carefully. "Thus the use of the concept of propitiation witnesses to two great realities, the one, the reality, and the seriousness of the divine reaction against sin, and the other, the reality and the greatness of the divine love which provided the gift which should avert the wrath from men."[20] Since "the idea of propitiation is the dominant note in the Wesleyan type of Arminian theology,"[21] this more detailed exposition is necessary.

(1) Biblical Concepts and Terminology (b) The New Testament (ii) Reconciliation

The word "reconciliation" is a term derived from the Greek verbs *katallasso* or *apokatallasso*, both of which mean, "to reconcile." In its scriptural usage it denotes a change from the state of enmity to one of favor or friendship. The Apostle Paul used the term several times. "For if, when we were enemies, we were reconciled to God by the death of his Son, much more, being reconciled, we shall be saved by his life. And not only so, but we also joy in God through our Lord Jesus Christ, by whom we have now received the atonement" (or reconciliation" A.S.V., *katallagen*, Romans 5:10,11; cf. 2 Corinthians 5:18, 19; Ephesians 2:16; Colossians 1:20-22). These passages clearly teach that we are reconciled to God by the death of His Son, though we need always to remember, "God was in Christ reconciling the world unto himself" (2 Corinthians 5:9a).

James Denney pointed out a significant phase of this term in its biblical usage. "The work of reconciliation, in the sense of the New Testament, is a work which is finished, and which we must conceive to be finished, before the gospel is preached."[22] However "this previous reconciliation of the world to Himself by the death of His Son," to which Denney alluded, "is to be distinguished also from 'the word of reconciliation' (cf. 2 Corinthians 5:19) which is to be proclaimed to the guilty, and by which they are entreated to be reconciled unto God,"[23] as H. Orton Wiley has stressed.

(1) Biblical Concepts and Terminology (b) The New Testament (iii) Redemption

This term comes from Greek verbs (*agorazo* and *exagorazo*), which literally means, "to purchase." Thus the emphasis is on the cost of our salvation to the Lord Jesus Christ. Sinful men are in bondage, "sold under sin" (Romans 7:14), "the bond-servant of sin" (John 8:34 ASV), and are under the curse of the law (Galatians 3:10). But "Christ hath redeemed us from the curse of the law, being made a curse for us: for it is written, 'Cursed is everyone that hangeth on a tree'" (Galatians 3:13, cf. 4:5, Revelation 5:9; 14:3, 4). A very closely related term is *ransom*, from *lutron*, which is literally "a means of loosing" (from *luo* to *loose*). It occurs only in two phrases in the New Testament—"to give his life a ransom in the place of many" (Mark 10:25; Matthew 20:28; lit.), and "who gave himself a substitute-ransom in the place of many" (1 Timothy 2:6, lit.). These three passages consistently indicate that the ransom was provisionally universal, while being of a vicarious character, "yet it is actual for those only who accept God's conditions, and who are described in the Gospel statements as 'the many.'"[24]

The Meaning of the Blood

Three words in Hebrews 9:7, "not without blood," represent forcibly the prominence given to the blood throughout Scripture, both Old and New Testament. "There is a marvelous unity of plan going through the Bible, and right at the center of that unity is the principle, 'Without shedding of blood there is no remission of sins.'"

The term "blood" has been a difficulty, if not great offense to many, aggravated undoubtedly by the literal and materialistic emphasis of some very earnest but mistaken Christians. Two important observations are necessary: (1) The emphasis on the blood of Christ in the New Testament is derived from the Old Testament. (2) The phrase, "the blood of Christ" is a metaphor, or spiritual language, not literal. On the occasion when Jesus spoke to the Jews about the necessity of eating His flesh and drinking His blood in order to have eternal life and enter into living union with Him, His words were received by them with a crass literalism. Jesus corrected this notion with these words: "The flesh profiteth nothing; the words that I speak unto you, they are spirit, and they are life" (John 6:63). An application of this statement to the New Testament references concerning "the precious blood of Christ" would save many from a great deal of misunderstanding. It is not the material substance that avails anything, but what the blood represents and symbolizes, namely, death and life.[25]

In the Book of Leviticus God Himself has defined His terms and provided His own commentary in regard to "the blood," "For the life of the flesh is in the blood: and I have given it to you upon the altar to make an atonement for your souls; for it is the blood that maketh an atonement for the soul ...For it is the life of all flesh; the blood of it is for the life thereof: therefore I said unto the children of Israel, Ye shall eat the blood of no manner of flesh: for the life of all flesh is the blood thereof" (17:11,14). Thus, blood means life, and blood shed means life poured out in behalf of sinners for redemptive purposes.[26] Blood not only witnesses to the violent death experienced by our Lord, it speaks also of His suffering of body and soul when He "was made sin for us who knew no sin" (2 Corinthians 5:21). There is no other cure. "There could be no access to God, no return to the heavenly sanctuary, for Jesus *as our representative*, without blood that fully answered for our sin. In the sacrifice of Himself He discovered the eternal redemption, and with that, 'through his own blood, entered in once for all into the holy place.'"[27] Thus blood, in its scriptural meaning, vividly symbolizes remission of sin, ransom, propitiation, justification, redemption, cleansing, and victory.

The Godward Aspects

The biblical terms already observed, propitiation, reconciliation, and redemption, are used in scripture to set forth the atonement in a three-fold manner: (1) in relation to God; (2) in relation to God and man; and (3) in relation to man. Thus, propitiation deals with the divine aspect of the atonement; reconciliation with the double aspect of its Godward and manward relations; and redemption with the manward aspect.[28]

In the propitiatory aspect of the atonement, the death of Christ is a sufficient sacrifice for the remission of sins, and the full satisfaction to the claims of divine justice. However, since God provided the atonement or propitiatory offering, He must be regarded as both the Reconciler and the Reconciled. "Man was created both as dependent upon God and as a free and responsible creature. The atonement satisfies both of these relations" (cf. 2 Corinthians 5:18,19).[29] Divine Love has freely and fully devised the plan through the incarnation and atonement for the breaking down of all the barriers between God and man. Hence reconciliation refers also to the state of peace existing between God and man (Romans 5:11). Through Calvary's Cross, the enmity between man and God was slain, as well as the enmity between man and man (cf. Ephesians 2:14-16; vs. 16 "And that he might reconcile both unto God in one body by the cross, having slain the enmity thereby").

T. C. Hammond gives an excellent four-fold summary of the Godward aspect of the atonement.[30] (a) Towards God, "the

Atonement is the supreme event in the world's history." It is described as giving God "pleasure," due chiefly to the perfect obedience of Christ, for it was the first time God's will, fully and entirely, had been "done on earth as it is in heaven." (b) "It demonstrated God's attributes of righteousness and love." There is no conflict between God's attributes. God's justice and His love are in no way opposed, for "the remission of sins is as much derived from His justice as His love." At Calvary's Cross, "Mercy and truth met together, righteousness and peace have kissed each other" (Psalm 85:10). (c) "It vindicated God as the Lawgiver." The moral wrong committed by sinful men in defiance of Divine law is both a stain on, and an affront to, the honor of the Lawgiver. However, the Redeemer's perfect obedience, extending even to His voluntary submission to death, vindicated the Lawgiver. At the Cross, Jesus Christ assumed our "legal liability," and gave full satisfaction to the Upholder of the moral laws of the Universe, and vindicated the Divine government. (d) Finally, "it secured a satisfactory basis for the remission of sins." The satisfaction provided in the redeeming work of Christ is sufficient for the penalty of sin. The intrinsic value of His sacrifice, which removes the sinner's legal liability when accepted by Him, stems from the infinite worth of Christ's own Person.

The Manward Aspects

Redemption for men has both objective and subjective aspects. Objectively, the entire race is provisionally redeemed in that the purchase price has been paid for all mankind. Subjectively, in relation to the individual, redemption is provisional and is made effective only through faith in the atoning death of Christ.

The blood of Christ is the ransom price for man's redemption. It secured for mankind a four-fold deliverance; (a) from the curse of the law (Galatians 3: 13); (b) from the law itself (Galatians 4:4, 5, cf. Romans 6:14); (c) from the power of sin (John 8:34; d. Romans 6:12-23); and (d) from the power of Satan (Hebrews 2:15). In the Wesleyan position, deliverance from the "bondage to sin" means experientially that we are redeemed from (a) the guilt of sin; (b) the reigning power of sin; and (c) from the inbeing of sin. The first results in justification, the second in regeneration, and the third in entire sanctification.[31]

Further, the sufferings of Christ are the greatest and strongest exhibition of God's love for man, and at the same time, indicate the enormity of man's sin and rebellion. Both of these factors, converging on the conscience of the sinner, bring the greatest possible constraint to repent and believe in Christ, and also become a transforming power within him. "Hereby perceive we the love of God, because he laid down his life for us" (1 John 3:16; cf. Romans 5:8; 1 John 4:19).

Representative Theories of the Atonement

Throughout the centuries various theories of the atonement have been advanced, but none of them have won universal acceptance. The variety of these theories indicates the numerous facets of the atonement, as well as the essential mystery and depth of the atonement. Briefly, the classical, or older types can be summarized under five headings.

The Ransom Theory

The Ransom Theory is the oldest of the types, in which the death of Christ is viewed as the divine effort to rescue men from the power of sin, death, and Satan. This view was advanced by Irenaeus (c. 200?) and Origen (185-254), and given classical expression by Gregory of Nyssa (c. 395). It held sway for a thousand years. It has been revived and restated in recent times by Gustaf Aulen and Sydney Cave.

The Satisfaction Theory

The Satisfaction Theory was put forward by Anselm in the eleventh century. This view insisted that man's sin was an affront to God's honor, and that Christ's death was a satisfaction to the wounded and outraged honor of God. It is sometimes called the "Objective Theory" since it grounded the atonement in the Divine Nature.

The Moral Influence

The Moral Influence Theory of Abelard appeared in the early part of the twelfth century. Peter Lombard expressed its substance in these words. "So great a pledge of love having been given to us, we are both moved and kindled to love God who did such great things for us. The death of Christ therefore justifies us, inasmuch as through it charity is stirred in our hearts."[32] It is referred to as the "Subjective Theory" for the work of Christ is interpreted as the revelation in word and deed of the forgiving love of God, with an emphasis upon the subjective effects that this revelation has on the sinner.

The Forensic Theory

The Forensic Theory of the Reformers, chiefly John Calvin, and their successors, viewed Christ's death as penal in nature. They regarded the work of Christ as a satisfaction in the sense of a penal substitution for the sinner. It is also called the Penal or Judicial Theory. Calvinists regarded the death of Christ as an exact penalty for the elect had they been lost.

The Governmental Theory

The Governmental Theory is associated with the name of Hugo Grotius (1583-1645). For Grotius the atonement was necessary to uphold the authority of God's law and government. Later, with some modifications, the theory was advocated by Richard Watson, the early Methodist theologian, and in more recent times, it was advocated by John Miley, also a Methodist.

Other theories have been formulated in the modern period. The Ethical Theory of A. H. Strong, a Baptist theologian, grounds the atonement in the holiness of God and the necessity of meeting an ethical demand of the Divine Nature. The Racial Theory of Olin Curtis, a Methodist theologian, regards the sufferings of Christ as the Race-Man, and the redeemed through Christ as the new humanity or race as the ultimate objective of the atonement. Gustaf Aulen, a present day Lutheran theologian of Sweden, champions what he calls the Classic doctrine of the atonement, which views the Cross as the victory of Christ over sin, evil, death, and Satan. This view has strong affinities with the Ransom Theory of the early Christian era. Finally, we note the Cosmic Theory of the atonement, as represented by Karl Heim, in which the dimensions of the atonement are given cosmic significance.

There is an element of truth in each of the theories of the atonement, even in those, which would be considered most inadequate from a biblical point of view. The defect of some theories (e.g. The Moral Influence Theory) inheres in the effort to present total truth from a limited or partial premise. The various theories, however, are testimony to the vastness and depth of the atonement, which ultimately defies any thoroughly adequate human formulation.

The Extent of the Atonement

It's Scope

Wesleyan Arminian theologians have always insisted upon the universality of the atonement. This does not mean that all men will be unconditionally or ultimately saved, but it does mean that God's provision through the sacrificial death of Christ is such as to make salvation a possibility for all. In the provisional sense, redemption is universal or general; in its application to the individual, it is special or conditional.

Four classes of Scripture passages can be cited to indicate that the atonement is universal in scope. (1) Those passages which declare that Christ died for all men: John 3:16, 17; 2 Corinthians 5: 14, 15; Hebrews 2:9; 1 John 2:2; 4:14. (2) Those passages which urge the universal proclamation of the Gospel to all men; Matthew 24:14; 28:19; Mark 16:15; Luke 24:47. (3) Those passages which bind the necessity of repentance upon all men; Acts 17:30, 31; 2 Peter 3:9; cf. Luke 13:3, (4) Those passages which state that Jesus Christ died for some who, in spite of His loving provisions, may perish: Rom. 14:15; 1 Corinthians 8:11.

Another aspect of the scope of salvation should be mentioned in that Christ died for His Church or His people with a definite purpose in view. His death encompasses an uttermost salvation in this world. "...Christ also loved the church, and gave himself for it; That he might sanctify and cleanse it with the washing of water by the word, That he might present it to himself a glorious church, not having spot, or wrinkle, or any such thing; but that it should be holy and without blemish" (Ephesians 5:25-27). "Wherefore Jesus also, that he might sanctify the people with his own blood, suffered without the gate" (Hebrews 13:12). Therefore the provisions of Christ's atoning death comprehends a "Free Salvation For All

Men and a Full Salvation From All Sin," as the motto of the Asbury institutions in Wilmore, Kentucky, declares.

It's Benefits

The gracious benefits of the atonement are two-fold in classification: (1) Unconditional and (2) Conditional.

The unconditional benefits include (a) the continued existence of the race; (b) the restoration of all men to a state of salvability; and (c) the salvation of those who die in infancy, or those who never develop to moral accountability.

The conditional benefits of the atonement are (a) justification, (b) regeneration, (c) adoption, (d) the witness of the Holy Spirit, (e) entire sanctification, and (f) glorification.

The death of Christ on Calvary's Cross was no morbid futile act. It is God's sufficient answer of love to the supreme need of the world.

> Love found a way to redeem my soul,
> Love found a way that could make me whole;
> Love sent my Lord to the cross of shame,
> Love found a way, O praise His holy name.

Divine love saw the alienation of sin, and found a way of reconciliation. Divine love saw the guilt of sin, and found a way of pardon. Divine love saw the depravity of sin, and found a means of restoration. Divine love saw the condemnation of sin, and found a method of justification. Divine love saw the defilement of sin and found a way of cleansing. Divine love saw the death of sin, and found a way of eternal life. Divine love saw, and sought, and found. The Lord of life Himself stepped from behind the veil of His eternal glory, appeared among men, died on a Cross of wood, rose again from the dead, ascended to the Father, and by so doing will bring "many sons unto glory" (Hebrews 2:10). It is this message that needs to be declared with faithfulness and urgency until He comes again!

Notes

---

[1] James Denney, *The Death of Christ* (New York: Hodder & Stoughton, n. d.), p. 283.

[2] D. M. Baillie, *God Was In Christ* (New York: Charles Scribner's Sons, 1948), p. 194. Quoted from Charles Allen Dinsmore.

[3] Vincent Taylor, *The Cross of Christ* (London: Mac-Millan & Co. Ltd. 1957), p. 87. Cf. Jasper Abraham Huffman, "The Meaning of the Cross" in *The Meaning of Things* (Winona Lake: The Standard Press, 1953), pp. 45-59; Herschel M. Hobbs, "The Meaning of the Death of Christ," *Christianity Today*, II:12:11-13 (Mar. 17, 1958).

[4] "The atonement is the satisfaction made to God for the sins of all mankind, original and actual, by the mediation of Christ, and especially by His passion and death, so that pardon might be granted to all while the divine perfections are kept in harmony, the authority of the Sovereign is upheld, and the strongest motives are brought to bear upon sinners to lead them to repentance, to faith in Christ, the necessary conditions of pardon, and to a life of obedience, by the gracious aid of the Holy Spirit." H. Orton Wiley, *Christian Theology* (Kansas City: Beacon Hill Press, 1947), II:271.

[5] (1) *God Loves*: "For God so loved the world..."; (2) *God Gives*: "that he gave his only begotten Son"; (3) *God Invites*: "that whosoever believeth in him"; (4) *God Saves*: "should not perish, but have everlasting life." John 3:16 is *Love's Good News*.

[6] Wiley, *op. cit.,* p. 228.

[7] Taylor, *op. cit.,* p. 85. Cf. Martin Werner "The Atonement As Moral Example" *The Christian Century* LXXVIII: 1232-1234 (Oct. 18, 1961): "Jesus...in his public message, addressed to all the people, the idea of a vicarious atonement through the surrender of his life plays no part at all." P. 1232. Also cf. G. W. Bromiley, "Substitution," *Christianity Today*; 1:13:5-7 (April 1, 1957).

[8] Cf. R. W. Dale, *The Atonement* (London: Congregational Union of England & Wales, 1909), pp. 499-505.

[9] Cf. John S. Banks, *A Manual of Christian Doctrine* (Cincinnati: Jennings & Graham, 1911), pp. 191-193; Wiley, *op. cit.,* pp. 228, 229; Leon Morris, "The Atonement," *Basic Christian Doctrines*, Carl F. H. Henry, ed. (New York: Holt, Rinehart and Winston, 1962), pp. 155-156; Bromiley, *op. cit.,* pp. 5, 6.

[10] Denny, *op. cit.,* pp. 324, 325.

[11] Cf. Henry C. Thiessen, *Lectures in Systematic Theology* (Grand Rapids: Wm. B. Eerdmans Publishing Company, 1951), pp. 312-315; William Evans, *The Great Doctrines of the Bible* (Chicago: The Moody Press, 1912, 1939), pp. 69-71.

[12] Evans, *op. cit.,* p. 70.

[13] R. A. Torrey, *What the Bible Teaches* (New York: Fleming H. Revell Company, 1898-1933), p. 144.

[14] Wiley, *op. cit.,* p. 185.

[15] Taylor, *op. cit.,* p. 9.

[16] H. E. Guillebaud, *Why the Cross?* (London: InterVarsity Fellowship, 1954), p. 130.

[17] Leon Morris, *The Apostolic Preaching of the Cross* (Grand Rapids: Wm. B. Eerdmans Pub. Co. 1956) p. 131.

[18] Roger Nicole, "Propitiation," *Christianity Today*, I:14:8 (April 15, 1957).

[19] William Burt Pope, *A Compendium of Christian Theology* (London: Wesleyan Conference Office, 1877), II: 272.

[20] Morris, *op. cit.,* p. 183.

[21] Wiley, *op. cit.,* p. 284.

[22] Denney, *op. cit.,* pp. 114, 145.

[23] Wiley, *op. cit.,* pp. 231, 232.

[24] W. E. Vine, *Expository Dictionary of New Testament Words* (London: Oliphants Ltd., 1957), III: 247, 248.

[25] Guillebaud, *op. cit.,* p. 137.

[26] Cf. J. C. Macaulay, *Devotional Studies in the Epistle to the Hebrews* (Wm. B. Ferdmans Pub. Co., 1949), pp. 139-147; Guillebaud, "The Meaning of the Blood of Christ," *op. cit.,* pp. 136-140; J. Marcellus Kik, "Offense of the Blood," *Christianity Today,* I:13:14-16 (April 1, 1957); Leon Morris, "The Blood-Life or Death?" *Christianity Today* II: 12:6-8 (March 17, 1958).

[27] Macaulay, *op. cit.,* p. 142.

[28] Wiley, *op. cit.,* p. 290.

[29] *Ibid.,* p. 291.

[30] T. C. Hammond, *In Understanding Be Men* (London: Inter-Varsity Fellowship, 1956), p. 125.

[31] Wiley, *op. cit.,* pp. 293, 294.

[32] Taylor, *op. cit.,* p. 72.

The Witness of the Spirit

Harold B. Kuhn

Sensitive Christians of all ages have been concerned with the question, "May I have assurance with respect to my acceptance before God?" The question persists and survives all attempts at halfway answers and quasi-explanations. The tendency of the Reformation to crystallize into glacial formulations of systems or to settle into the dull groove of liturgy and formalism resulted in movements of quest for inner certainty, at least as early as the seventeenth century. Prior to the movement initiated by the Wesleys, the Moravians and the Quakers in particular were formulating teachings concerning Christian assurance. Something will be noted later of the more detailed manner in which these two groups contributed to the thought of Wesley in this respect. For the moment, it should be noted that the desire for certainty is as old as the human spirit itself. It is not therefore surprising that the New Testament should contain clear-cut teachings at this point. It is surprising, on the other hand, that Christianity has historically made so little of the doctrine of the Witness of the Spirit.

Medieval Christianity was, of course, hindered in this respect by its highly institutional character, by which the forgiveness of sins was regarded as the prerogative of the Church. As a result, the communication of the assurance of salvation became the function of the absolving priest. It was not easy for the churches of the Reformation to find a scriptural equivalent of this medieval conception. At the same time, it should have been remembered that the Bible strongly teaches that the Holy Spirit has a ministry of comfort and assurance to man precisely at the points where his need is felt to be the greatest.

Before turning to the manner in which the doctrine of the Witness of the Spirit developed as part of the heritage of Protestantism, we do well to observe the manner in which the Wesleyan awakening fits into the thought world into which it came. It should be borne in mind that the eighteenth century was the century of Reason. One of the features of this Enlightenment was a deep distrust of any expression of man's inner life. To the typical Man of Reason, any such consideration as that of "assurance of salvation" was regarded as fanaticism or "enthusiasm" and as such to be condemned roundly.

It appears clear, therefore, that if the Wesleyan movement had been simply a movement of the human spirit, then it ought not to have taken its rise in the eighteenth century at all. The Wesleys stood against the major thought currents of their times in such a manner that, viewed from the stand-point of mere history, their movement ought to have died on the vine. The times could not have been less favorable, humanly speaking, for its rise and spread—and yet it arose in one of the centers of formal learning, and soon spread and grew mightily in the England of Rationalism and Deism.

Seldom, then, has history borne witness to a more clearly evident operation of the grace of God against the trends of the age. And the work of John Wesley had for its very cutting edge a doctrine, which challenged the dryness and sterility of a merely rational approach to life and its problems, namely, the doctrine of the Witness of the Spirit. This doctrine, you see, declared the validity of an inward response to outward grace, a response that touched the emotions as well as the mind. Seldom has there been a movement in history, which was more clearly authenticated as being a movement of the Holy Spirit than this; and it is the doctrine now under study, which most vividly challenged the spirit of the eighteenth century.

Historical Rootage of the Doctrine

The Wesleyan doctrine of the Witness of the Holy Spirit must be regarded, not as a teaching which sprang into existence full grown in the eighteenth century, but as a logical and legitimate extension of principles which, however neglected, were long characteristic of the Christian message in its broad and general sense. It is good, therefore, to set the specific doctrine in its larger context. Scripturally this context is expressed in the language of St. Paul in 1 Corinthians 2:12; "Now we have received, not the spirit of the world, but the spirit which is of God; that we might know the things that are freely given to us of God." This passage embeds the principle, that God's bestowals upon men through the Holy Spirit are confirmed or authenticated by the same Spirit. To use language more typical of our time, God desires to communicate the awareness of His gifts, quite as much as He delights to bestow the gifts themselves.

The presuppositions of this are several: first, that the Holy Spirit has access directly to the mental processes of human beings; second, that this access is of such a nature that not only impressions but content can be communicated; and third, that the authentication of God's gifts proceed from the same source as the gifts themselves. These propositions, which will be noted in detail later, may not be taken for granted in our time, certainly not in circles which are influenced by the newer studies in semantics and which are suspicious of all attempts at verbalization of religious truth. It needs likewise to be said that in some Evangelical circles, there are those who regard the teaching of the Spirit's witness to justification as presumption or as claiming to know too much. Sensitive Christians will recognize, of course, that any tracing of the ways of the Holy Spirit constitutes a delicate study, one which touches deep mysteries in God's ways no less than in man's responses.

It may come as a surprise to many in the Wesleyan tradition to find that the subject of the Spirit's testimony to the human soul was a concern of the sixteenth century Reformers, particularly John Calvin. True, Calvin applied the teaching in a manner quite other than it has found application in Wesleyan circles. To him, the major subject upon which the Holy Spirit brought an inwardly persuading witness to bear upon human hearts was that of the certainty and authority of the Christian Revelation. He developed the teaching of the *testimonium spiritus sancti*, by which was meant that as God gives the Bible through the inspiration of the sacred writers, He also gives a certification that it is Revelation. In his elaboration of this doctrine, Calvin sought to correct the error of Roman Catholicism, which located the source of the testimony to Revelation in a Church which was assumed to be infallible, and at the same time, to give boundaries to what he felt to be fanatical claims for individual revelations which might or might not be harmonious with Scripture.

Calvin felt that Rome concealed the Word under the weight of traditional rubble; he felt that mystics and enthusiasts separated the Word from the Spirit. Both failed to do justice to the union of Word and Spirit by which the external (i.e., written) Word was internalized by the persuasive manifestation within the regenerate human consciousness of its vitality and authority. Calvin's teaching gave rise to the coarse jest involving the Dominican who was said to have held the Bible to his ear and to have heard nothing. This is of course a caricature of the great Reformer's teaching, which emphasized that the Holy Spirit impressed the conviction of the validity of the Scriptures upon the *believing* heart, the inward certainty that they were the Word of Life.

It might be remarked at this point, that it was this interpretation of the Witness of the Spirit (or perhaps better, the interpretation of this phase of that Witness), which has given to the churches in the Reformed tradition their high estimate of the Bible as the Word of God. This is an emphasis to which churches in the Wesleyan. Arminian tradition might well give serious attention.

Martin Luther likewise believed that God by the Holy Spirit attended the Word, which He had given. Luther was concerned especially to show the manner in which the Holy Spirit, through the Word, lifts Christ from the realm of the merely historical and makes Him vitally real to the inner consciousness of the believer. In Luther, moreover, the witness of the Holy Spirit to Revelation blended rather normally with the Spirit's testimony to the certainty of the believer's acceptance with God. He opposed, of course, the Roman Catholic assertion that only the Church can give assurance of personal salvation. To him, this assurance rested upon the deeper certainty of the revelation embodied in the Scriptures.

In his *Commentary on Galatians* Luther writes:

The Holy Ghost is sent by the Word into the hearts of the believers, as here it is said, 'God sent the spirit of his son,' etc. This sending is without any visible appearance; to wit, when, by the hearing of the external word, we receive an inward fervency and light, whereby we are changed and become new creatures, whereby

> we also receive a new judgment, a new feeling,
> and a new moving.[1]

From this it is clear that Luther sensed, if perhaps from afar, the reality of the Spirit's ability to provide "a new judgment," a new response to the reality of the new relationship, which is set up in justification. It goes without saying that the doctrine of the Witness of the Spirit is not to be found in Luther in the fully developed form, which it assumes in the Wesleyan literature of the eighteenth century. But it is noteworthy that Wesley was reading Luther's *Commentary on Galatians* in the weeks preceding May 24, 1738.[2]

It must be remembered that Luther was restrained in his statements at this point, due in part to the manner in which some, almost from the inception of the Reformation, tended to fanaticism, for some felt themselves so illuminated that they could safely neglect the Bible. This may be a logical outcome of the freeing of the human spirit, which ensued as the Church was liberated from the authoritarianism of the Medieval Church, but it contained within itself its own perils. Luther perceived these; and they probably hindered him from exploring the question as fully as he would otherwise have done.

It needs to be noted in this connection that objectors have attacked the teaching of both Luther and Calvin at this point on the grounds that it leads to fanaticism. David F. Strauss was particularly emphatic at this point in the nineteenth century. His contention was that the logical outcome of the teaching was that no Scripture was needed, since the Witness supplants the Spirit. This fails to take into account the fact that the *testimonium* is not in itself the authority, but that it only certifies or authenticates the embodiment of authority.

Enough has been said to indicate that the major questions involved in the discussion of the Wesleyan aspect of the doctrine of the Witness of the Spirit were raised by the earlier reformers. The willingness of God to certify His work belongs to the core of Protestantism. And that this certification should be understood as operating in more than one direction is significant, in that it represents a growing movement toward the articulation of the truth which underlies the erroneous attempts by Roman Catholicism to offer institutional and presumably infallible authentication at several vital points.

Something ought to be noted here concerning the manner in which two movements of the time just preceding that of Mr. Wesley had their influence upon him. It is well known that he felt strongly the testimony of Peter Boehler of the Moravian movement. While Wesley did not find himself in full agreement with the Moravian theology as elaborated by Count Zinzendorf, he did come to the position (slowly it is true) held by Boehler that "a true living faith in Christ is inseparable from a sense of pardon for all past and freedom from all present sins."[3]   Thus, although Boehler departed for Carolina for missionary service some days before the experience of Mr. Wesley at Aldersgate, he left behind him in the mind and heart of the scholar of Epworth and of Lincoln College a deep desire for a personal sense of forgiveness, an undeniable desire to know the spirit's witness for himself.

While Mr. Wesley seldom mentions George Fox or the movement of Quakerism in his writings, there are similarities between the teachings of George Fox and that of Wesley at this point, which cannot be explained as being mere coincidences. The Quakers had by 1740 impressed deeply upon the consciousness of religious England the principle that true Christian faith issues in a type of vibrant and joyous assurance of salvation. In a memorable passage, George Fox said: "...then I heard a voice which said, there is one, even Christ Jesus, that can speak to thy condition; and when I heard it, my heart did leap for joy."[4]

The teaching of the Spirit's ministry at this point was not elaborated systematically by Fox or Robert Barclay. However, the reality was there, and the success of the early Quaker movement, particularly in the Midlands of England, can scarcely be imagined apart from the message of joyous assurance, which the Friends bore. This message was published widely between 1652 and 1730; and the climate which it produced in English society in general no doubt served to produce the fine state of receptivity to the ministry of the Wesleys and their band of lay preachers in the mid-eighteenth century.

Turning to the specifically Wesleyan understanding of the Witness of the Spirit, one should note at the outset that John Wesley sought to avoid any over-simplification of the subject—that is, he saw the problem as one requiring careful definition and precise delineation. He divided the Witness into two parts, the direct and the indirect. The classic Scripture for this is, of course, Romans 8:16: "The Spirit himself beareth witness with our spirit, that we are the children of God." It has been suggested that this passage accords with the Old Testament proviso, that in the mouth of two or three witnesses should a truth be established.

Before turning to the consideration of these "two witnesses" let us note that they operate jointly. The first is "with" the second. The suggestion is, of course, that the two serve as either confirming or correcting each other. It is only as they confirm a common fact that their joint testimony is to be regarded as valid. It is this emphasis, which has given to the doctrine of the Witness of the Spirit as defined by John Wesley its characteristic sanity and balance. It was this which shored up the Wesleyan movement from the exaggerated subjectivism which Wesley felt to be characteristic of much of continental pietism, notably that of the Moravians. Mr. Wesley appreciated the contribution, which Peter Boehler made to his own life at this point, but he saw the dangers inherent in the Moravian emphasis upon inward experience, without proper "checks and balances."

In his monumental sermon, "The Witness of the Spirit," John Wesley says: "How many have mistaken the voice of their own imagination for this witness of the Spirit of God, and thence idly presumed they were the children of God, while they were doing the work of the devil! These are truly and properly enthusiasts; and, indeed, in the worse sense of the word."[5] From this, it is clear that he had met and crossed verbal swords with "enthusiasts" who had based their feeling of security upon an unchecked and untested witness. He noted, further, that when once they have been thus misled, it is almost impossible to show them their mistake. He feels that a misreading of the facts at this point places them "far above all the usual methods of conviction."

It is understandable also, that when some saw the error into which some were led with respect to this doctrine, they repudiated it entirely, and resorted to the opposite extreme of insisting that any clear authentication of one's acceptance with God is impossible in this life. Mr. Wesley suggests in his sermon a middle course namely, that we "keep a sufficient distance from that spirit of error and enthusiasm, without denying the gift of God and giving up the great privilege of his children."[6]

It has been noted thus far that the basic principle, which underlies the doctrine of the Witness of the Spirit, is, that the God who bestows His gifts also stands willing to authenticate them. Attention has been given to the way in which the earlier reformers applied the principle of the Spirit's witness, primarily to the authentication of the Word, but secondarily (in Luther) to the assurance of personal adoption. And it has been observed that the Witness is two-fold in its application, this interpretation being agreeable to Scripture, and significant in the safeguarding of the Witness itself against misinterpretation and presumption.

In the discussion which follows, there will be noted, first, the nature of the direct witness of the Spirit. Following this, attention will be given to the indirect witness "of our spirit"; and finally, there will be discussion of the spiritual significance of this great doctrine.

The Direct Testimony of the Spirit

First and most basic to the consideration of the direct witness of the Spirit is the principle that the purposes of God conform in their expression to one overall purpose. That is, there is one central objective discernible in the activity of God in the saving of man, namely, that "the man of God may be perfect, thoroughly furnished unto all good works." This determines the extent and quality of applied redemption, and carries with it as a clear corollary that the awareness appropriate to personal salvation should be conveyed to the one who has been reached by Grace. Thus, it is the same Father who convicts and convinces of sin, who calls effectively to salvation, who justifies and regenerates, and who initiates the procedures by which the one "justified by faith" enters into newness of life.

Just as "God was in Christ reconciling the world unto Himself," so also it is the Father's good pleasure to give men the Kingdom, and thus the Holy Spirit is designated by the same Father to make known to us, individually and inwardly, the things freely dispensed to us. The Holy Spirit thus expresses, in speaking to men, the mind and purposes of the Father. He thus also is the bearer of the Good Tidings that follow justification by faith. Justification is an action which passes in the mind of the Father; and as Mr. Wesley says in his famous sermon, "Justification by Faith," "...the judgment of the all wise God is always according to truth."[7] Thus justification is, according to Mr. Wesley, "that act of God the Father whereby, for the sake of the propitiation made by the blood of his Son, he 'showeth forth his righteousness (or mercy) by the remission of the sins that are past.'"[8]

It is upon the basis of this justification that the Holy Spirit bears witness to majestic fact: He objectifies that which is in the mind and heart of the Father. Sharing in the divine omniscience, He takes the tidings of the Father's gift and conveys it to His child. It is this sharing of the Father's mind which authenticates the Witness of the Spirit.

A second principle, which underlies the Spirit's witness, is that He has access to the inner processes of man. It is not difficult to understand that men of the eighteenth century regarded such an assertion as an expression of "enthusiasm" and in some cases at least, of spiritual arrogance. There seems to be a built-in objection upon the part of men blinded by the god of this world to the possibility of clear and direct communication of the assurance of salvation. This is not the place to analyze this objection in detail. It belongs to the discussion rather to point out that the access of the Holy Spirit to the inner mental processes is usually regarded as a possibility in a negative, but not in a positive, sense. That is to say, few will deny that the Holy Spirit has the capability of bringing pressure to bear upon lost men at the point of their non-acceptance and their disharmonious relation with God.

It is singular that the ability of the Holy Spirit to convict and convince of guilt and of alienation is so easily recognized and accepted, while at the same time it is thought a thing impossible that He should be able to be the bearer of good tidings. We suggest it as a principle, that just as His access to the inner life makes it possible for Him to bring sinners to distress and to the anguish of lostness, so that same access makes it possible for Him to convince the justified that their guilt is cancelled, and that their reconciliation has been made a fact. Mr. Wesley puts it thus: "The testimony now under consideration is given by the Spirit of God to and with our spirit; he is the person testifying. That he testifies to us is, 'that we are the children of God.'"[9]

Of the nature of this inward persuasion, Mr. Wesley says again:

> I do not mean hereby, that the Spirit of God testifies this by any outward voice; no, nor always by an inward voice, although he may do this sometimes. Neither do I suppose, that he always applies to the heart (though he often may) one or more tests of Scripture. But he so works upon the soul by his immediate influence, and by a strong though inexplicable operation, that the stormy wind and troubled waves subside, and there is a sweet calm.[10]

It follows that the precise means is not the important thing; the precise nature of the media is secondary to the fact. Men and women may live with many forms of uncertainty; but in this one all-significant area, God does not intend that there shall be the harrowing and gnawing problem of suspense and doubt.

It needs to be noted also that the Spirit's witness is subject to a number of variables, a number of diversities, which are rooted in the range of individual differences in temperament and response. In a most general sense, it may be laid down as a principle that the Holy Spirit "cuts with the grain," that is, He operates within the context of the usually discernible principles of human knowledge and human learning. Usually also He works in a manner conformable to the customary responses of the individual. This means that the response of the person who is accustomed to react with vigor and great enthusiasm to any bit of good news may be expected frequently to sense the Spirit's witness in terms appropriate to his usual pattern of response. On the other hand, the individual who is by nature and practice phlegmatic and unexpressive may frequently sense the Spirit's testimony as a *quiet inward persuasion*, an inner conviction that it is "well with his soul."

In some cases, which may be regarded as exceptions to the rule but without being highly exceptional, the Spirit's witness breaks through the usual patterns of response. The ebullient and effervescent person finds this deep reality in terms of the solemn inner persuasion, while the more steady moving person may find himself responding in a manner, which is surprising to himself for its warmth and felt-graciousness. The important thing to be borne in mind within the Wesleyan tradition is, that just as the Almighty has regard for individual differences, so also we in dealing with individuals should afford the largest recognition and respect for differences in their patterns of response. One thing only is needful: that the reality be present. The precise manner in which this reality is conveyed is, in the final analysis, an affair which belongs to the One who knows all hearts, and who deals with individuals in terms of a comprehensive knowledge of all that has gone into their processes by way of heredity and conditioning.

Thus far we have noted some of the general principles, which underlie the consideration of the direct witness of the Spirit. That such a witness is the portion of the children of God seemed to Mr. Wesley indisputable. As he remarks, "None can deny this, without flatly contradicting the Scriptures, and charging a lie to God." Thus, there was no doubt in the mind of the great Wesleyan leader that the direct testimony of God's Spirit to the believer was clearly envisaged in the divine purposes, so that its reception might be regarded as normative for the justified believer.

With respect to the manner in which the witness is impressed upon the inner processes of the one receiving it, Mr. Wesley spoke with considerable reserve. After all, the "deep things of God" are not always reducible for purposes of communication to ordinary propositions. However, it will not suffice to regard the content of the Spirit's testimony as being nothing more than a mere subjective impression, without formal content. Content there must be if the testimony is to be instructive at all. At this point he says, "The testimony of the Spirit is an inward impression on the soul whereby the Spirit of God directly witnesses to my spirit, that I am a child of God; that Jesus Christ hath loved me, and given Himself for me; and that all my sins are blotted out, and I, even I, am reconciled to God."[11]

It will be helpful here to note the words with which Mr. Wesley here elaborates or goes beyond the words of Romans 8:16. First, the witness is an inward impression; it is intimate, personalized, and direct. It registers on the inner processes with an impact of news or tidings. The witness is individualized: the 'we' and the 'our' become 'I' and 'me'. It includes the ground and cause of that which is authenticated: it rests upon the facts, "that Jesus Christ hath loved me, and given himself for me." And it is brought to bear supremely on the fact "that all my sins are blotted out" so that "I, even I, am reconciled to God."

This appeals to us as being clearly derivable from Scripture; it accords with the most profound needs of the human spirit; it certifies the most significant fact, which can be brought home to any person. That is, into the inner sanctuary of the heart has come the voice of the Eternal One. It detracts nothing that the process of communication is mysterious; mystery is not damaging provided the normal processes of the inner life are left inviolate, and providing that the content accords with objective reality.

It goes without saying that this direct testimony of God's Spirit is not the result of a process of examination and inference. There may be place for these in connection with the "witness of our spirit"; but in the matter immediately under discussion, inference is not sufficient to banish the painful state of doubt and uncertainty which has, up to this moment, been aggravated by the processes which have led up to repentance. Not only so: but the frame of mind of the penitent affords a background of strong contrast, by which the Spirit's witness glows forth. His self-loathing, his feeling of helplessness, and his abandonment of any hope for saving himself produce such a climate within him that only something coming from outside himself can serve to dispel his doubts and remove his sense of alarm. It is at this point that the Spirit's testimony comes with such force. And it is a testimony, which is totally different from the inferences, which he has just been drawing from his own state and from the reasoning of his own spirit.

Thus, it is to be regarded as one of the very gracious provisions of the Heavenly Father that the Holy Spirit is sent to relieve this state of painful doubt and uncertainty in the penitent. No longer is he an orphan; no longer must he live in suspense with respect to his filial relation to the Father in Heaven. Doubt is excluded; the reality of sonship is borne in upon the consciousness, so that he can exult:

My God is reconciled
His pardoning voice I hear;

> He owns me as His child,
> I can no longer fear.
> With confidence I now draw nigh,
> And Father, Abba Father, cry.

Mr. Wesley saw in his day the necessity for throwing safeguards about the question of the precise manner in which the Spirit's witness is conveyed to the seeker. Certainly it was not to be expected that there would be an outward audible voice, nor yet could one insist upon the actual 'hearing' of an inward voice. Not necessarily, he suggests, must there be an application of a specific text of Scripture, although the Spirit may utilize this form. But the essential at this point is, that the inward conviction should be so impressed upon the soul that there is a certainty that the individual has indeed passed from death unto life. Hear his words:

> But He so works upon the soul by His immediate influence, and by a strong, though inexplicable operation, that the stormy wind and troubled seas subside, and there is a sweet calm, the heart resting as in the arms of Jesus, and the sinner being clearly satisfied that God is reconciled, that all his 'iniquities are forgiven, and his sins covered.'[12]

In this connection, it needs to be noted that the Witness of the Spirit is not something radically different from the faith, which justifies. In his letter in reply to Richard Tompson, he points out that "The assurance in question is no other than the full assurance of faith." [13] It goes without saying that this "full assurance of faith" is imparted by the Holy Spirit, and that it rests upon a prior repentance and turning of the soul unto God.

Something needs to be said concerning the matter of the maintenance of this direct witness within the soul. Mr.

Wesley maintained that the testimony of the Spirit could be lost through willful disobedience. This he based upon his belief that the sinful act also breaks the connection of faith. Presumably, therefore, the Spirit's witness is restored when the individual is restored, through repentance, from his disobedience. The foregoing accords with Mr. Wesley's disavowal of unconditional perseverance or unqualified "eternal security." He believes that the Witness of the Spirit may be so sustained and developed that it ripens into what he calls "The full assurance of hope," this being an advanced degree of persuasion which comes with maturity in Christian grace. He does not believe that this persuasion is held unconditionally, irrespective of obedience to the divine will. Rather, as one abides in holiness of life, this "full assurance" is graciously sustained. But there is never lacking the necessity for a responsible working together with God in obedience.

The Witness of the Human Spirit

One of the genuinely original contributions of John Wesley to the doctrine of the Witness of the Spirit was his careful relating of the *direct* and *indirect* testimonies. As we have noted, the teaching of a direct testimony of the Spirit was known prior to his time. Likewise, the basic test indicated in the words, "By their fruits ye shall know them," was scarcely a discovery of the eighteenth century. But the systematic exposition of the joint quality of the two "witnesses" was typically Wesleyan, and marks a significant advance in the history of Christian doctrine.

Just as the direct testimony of the Holy Spirit to the human soul is diversified and personalized, so also the indirect witness "of our own spirit" is affected by individual differences in response and apprehension. The constant element here is, that the appeal of the indirect witness is to the genuineness of the changed relation between the justified individual and his Lord. While the direct witness is to our spirit, and in the nature of the case stands on the evidence of God's own justifying pronouncement, independent of all other evidence, the indirect witness proceeds *from* our spirit, and rests upon the production of new graces and new dispositions. It follows that the time element will be different in the case of the latter from that of the former. Of this, notice will be taken later.

The witness of "our spirit" rests in the first instance upon that which has been done within us; there are certain marks of sonship, capable of being sensed and recognized. This makes it deeply significant that these tokens should be rightly understood and properly discovered. One is drawn at once to the list of the "fruit of the Spirit"; love, joy, peace, long-suffering, gentleness, goodness, faithfulness, meekness, and self control. Mr. Wesley was most emphatic in warning his hearers and readers against trying to rest in any alleged testimony of the Spirit, apart from the graces, which that same Spirit imparts. These graces are rightly regarded as the outcome of the change, which is produced in the inner life in what is commonly called "conversion."

It is obvious that this cluster of graces represents a large order, and that some might shrink from any profession of them, taken as a whole. Such persons might find it easier to recognize the element of over-all change, such as is suggested by St. Paul in 2 Corinthians 5:17; "Therefore if any man be in Christ he is a new creation." That is to say, some persons find it easier to recognize, especially in the early stages of their new life in Christ, the broad gauge alteration of life-pattern. Upon reflection such a person suddenly awakens to the realization: "I have been made new! My life has a new center of gravity. I have a new set of likes, a new set of dislikes. All things have become new!"

Thus, the pardoning love of God has stretched forth a hand, which is mighty, and has produced inward changes answerable to the need of one who has seen the enormity of sin and has turned with profound contrition away from it. This does not mean that the life of God in the soul, thus begun in what may be imperfect knowledge and which certainly begins in relative inexperience, may and will not need to develop in the area of the display of the graces of the Spirit. These may require exercise to become strong; but they are present, and they make their impact upon the awareness of the new Christian.

Another specific element in the recognition in the human spirit of the coming of "new life" is that of an alteration in the direction of the will. He who has looked into the nature of sin has seen the manner in which it has distorted the will, making the self its center and subject. He has seen the manner in which it asserts the human self as a low-grade sovereign, wearing a tinfoil crown, and imagining itself to be autonomous. One of the more obvious and easily discernible features of the regenerate life is that the human will is gladly yielded to the known will of the Heavenly Father. By this transformation, the new Christian can say from his inner being, and in a manner which corresponds to the light which he possesses, "I delight to do thy will, O my God: yea, thy law is within my heart." It would seem that this transposition of the center upon which the will is fixed is one of the most conspicuous and easily perceived changes that enter into the persuasion, which constitutes the testimony of "our spirit."

A further area in which the transformation which regeneration brings into the inner life occurs is that which relates to one's attitude toward spiritual and eternal things. One of the cardinal marks of the unregenerate life is its inveterate attachment to the world and its synthetic gods.

These have been the objects of continual and unquestioning pursuit; and the tawdry trifles that they offer, have been regarded as "status symbols" to be treasured and garnered. But now the new Christian finds that a new dimension has entered his life and thought, a dimension of eternity, which has modified and revised his scale of values. Temporal things begin to be seen for what they are: that is, they appear as a fleeting part of a life which has been subordinated to new and other ends. The regenerating Spirit has also brought a new gift of sight, whereby the believer looks "not at the things which are seen, but at the things which are not seen." This involves a revaluation of the visible and the temporal, which amounts to a vast overturn of values.

With respect to the relation of present-and-future, there is a similarly discernible change. Whereas in the former days, the present was regarded as the all-significant, and whereas the future was frequently by-passed as being too precarious (and hence to be pushed to the periphery of one's thought), now the present is discounted in favor of the future—and the unknown and formerly menacing aspects of that future are committed to One who "shall choose our inheritance for us." This is the newly engendered mood of the converted heart; it speaks the language of faith, and leaves the contingent and the mysterious of the future to a fatherly heart, in calm trust that what He chooses is best. Here faith blossoms into hope: and upon the basis of the mercies of the past, the child of God recognizes that the future, which will without doubt bring a blend of joy and sorrow, will yet be administered by One whose love has already brought much of joy, and who will without doubt synchronize the events of the days ahead in such a manner as to cause them to turn out for good. He is thus in a position to view the operation of the principle, that "all things work together for good to them that love God."

Another feature, which emerges as the new Christian lives with the new life in the Holy Spirit, is that of a new evaluation of persons. This is as vivid in its way as the new evaluation of things has been in its way. To a degree not always recognized, the unregenerate person views his fellow men as being placed here for his own advantage. Those who face the rough and tumble of today's business world know well the degree to which men and women of the world utilize others as ladders to their own success, to be kicked aside when the goal has been achieved. The Christian finds that the inward transformation which conversion has wrought in him changes this. Others become persons in their own right, worthy of recognition and respect. This, however, is in reality the minor element in the change of outlook; the major one is, that other men and women are recognized as potential children of God, who are, just as much as he himself, loved by an everlasting heart.

The Significance of the Witness of the Spirit to the Christian Today

The doctrine of the Witness of the Spirit has twofold significance to the Church of today. First, it represents a meaningful development in the history of Christian theology; and second, it speaks of one of the glorious privileges of the individual believer. This is not the place to discuss in detail the place of the doctrine in the history of Christian thought; but it needs to be noted that such a scholar as W. H. Griffith Thomas regards the Wesleyan emphasis upon the Witness of the Spirit as part of a movement of return to a full New Testament understanding of the Holy Spirit.[14] Arnold B. Come also suggests that this doctrine serves as an important theological corrective to one-sidedness in Christian emphasis, whether in the direction of a too-great objectivity, or whether in the direction of too much stress upon the inward, subjective phase.[15] Certainly its elaboration by Wesleyan scholars marks a distinct advance in the formulation of Christian theology.

More important to this discussion is the fact that the Witness of the Holy Spirit is one of the major privileges of the Christian believer – a privilege that may however be by-passed as a result of the lack of understanding. Mr. Wesley was both courageous and helpful in his assertion, in the face of much opposition, that the Spirit's witness was one of the New Testament "gifts of the Spirit" which did not and should not disappear with the end of New Testament times. As Lycurgus M. Starkey points out, he recognized that while there may have been charismata or spiritual gifts which were chiefly for apostolic times, that this is one of "those ordinary gifts and operations which every Christian is privileged to seek and receive."[16]

It is possible that one might be accepted of God and yet not possess the inward testimony of the Holy Spirit to that acceptance; but it is clear that the one who lacks this witness is deprived of something, which is very valuable and helpful to the living of the Christian life in our kind of a world. There is a calm confidence, a firmness of spiritual step, which is vital to triumphant living.

This testimony of the Spirit brings into the Christian heart a sense of certainty, which lays the groundwork for witnessing. Few can fail to be impressed by the calm testimony of a believer who "knows whom he has believed." Moreover, in this is to be found a valid application of the empirical method in the spiritual life; thoughtful persons have agreed that the Wesleyan appeal to experience is in accord with the best scientific thought of the times.[17]

It is true, moreover, that the times may be ripe for a renewed emphasis upon this doctrine in the Church at large.

During times when there is stress upon the external expressions of religion, the need for assurance tends to fall in the background;[18] but it is likely that the current stress upon liturgy in the non-liturgical churches will be short-lived, and men and women will turn with hungry hearts once again toward inward spiritual assurance. Evangelicals will do well to be sensitive to this probable turn of events. In the meantime, the need of the human heart for certainty is a perennial one. Whenever earnest souls turn to their Lord for deliverance, they deeply welcome the inward authentication of their acceptance with Him. It is to these "meek souls who will receive Him still" that He gives the word of assurance, the word of sonship and of acceptance.

Notes

1 Comment on Chapter IV, v. 6.

2 Arthur S. Yates, *The Doctrine of Assurance*, p. 56.

3 Nehemiah Curnock (ed), The Journal of the Rev. John Wesley, I, p. 472.

4 George Fox, *Journal*, Vol. I, Sec. 11.

5 W. P. Harrison (ed), *The Wesleyan Standards*, Vol. I, p. 201.

6 *Ibid.*, p. 202.

7 *Ibid.*, p. 107.

8 *Ibid.*, p. 108.

9 *Ibid.*, p. 220.

10 *Ibid.*, p. 221.

11 *Ibid.*, pp. 205f.

12 E. H. Sugden (ed), *Wesley's Standard Sermons*, II, p. 345.

13 Thomas Jackson (ed), *The Works of the Rev. John Wesley*, Vol. VIII, p. 283.

14 W. H. Griffith Thomas, *The Holy Spirit of God*, p. 113.

15 Arnold B. Come, *The Human Spirit and the Holy Spirit*, p. 175.

16 Lycurgus M. Starkey, Jr., *The Work of the Holy Spirit*, p. 76.

17 Townsend, Workman, and Eayrs, *New History of Methodism*, Vol. I, p. 27.

18 H. Wheeler Robinson, *The Christian Experience of the Holy Spirit*, p. 217.

The Doctrine of Sanctification

George A. Turner

The Nature of Sanctification

One of the central themes of the Scriptures is that God can make bad people good. He not only accounts or reckons believers as righteous but He can also actually change them so that they become transformed persons, recreated in "righteousness and true holiness" (Ephesians 4:24). The process by which God makes bad men into "saints" may be called sanctification; it should be a concern of anyone who desires to be better than he now is. No doctrine of sanctification is valid unless related to a sound doctrine of sin. One's understanding of the nature of sin is dependent, in turn, upon his doctrine of God. It was because the ancient Greeks had no adequate conception of God that they had such an inadequate idea of sin. Their gods were believed to practice deeds of which their worshippers were ashamed. Thus the gods were more vile than their worshippers. The Hebrews, however, believed God to be utterly holy and without sin. Because of this they believed that their God wanted His people to live victoriously above sin. To make such a statement, however, exposes one to the charge of believing in "perfectionism," of having what Reinhold Niebuhr calls pharisaical "pretentions to righteousness." In justification of such "pretentions" one may call to mind the brilliant study of this subject by a British scholar, who in 1927 published a study, which deserves a wide circulation. In it he noted that because the Israelites believed in a perfectly holy God they came to believe that God's people should be holy. This, in turn, led them to believe in a Messianic ruler whose reign would be characterized by utter righteousness. This in turn led them to expect a destiny in which holiness would be triumphant, sin banished, and virtue vindicated – a "new heaven and a new earth."[1]

Another Englishman once pled with his contemporaries that he be permitted to believe that if God said, "Ye shall be holy," it is possible to obey this command. Thus, John Wesley led the age long quest for holiness from the cloister to the mid-stream of life during the revolutionary period of the eighteenth century. In this age of space achievement, an age, which has penetrated to the inner secrets of the atom, an age, which is threatened with self-destruction, there ought to be a proper concern with essential righteousness. An age of general toleration ought at least to tolerate those who take seriously the quest for personal sanctity.

Perhaps the most convincing statement that the quest for holiness is a vain one was presented by a noted New Testament scholar and member of the translation committee of the Revised Standard Version. He wrote that "sanctification" in the New Testament is simply another term for justification, that it is never associated with the higher levels of Christian grace, and that the New Testament itself does not reflect a very high state of grace on the part of early Christian leaders.[2] In connection with this subject he expressed doubt that the Revised Standard Version should have changed the language of the 1952 printing from "consecrate" to "sanctify" in several places.

Sanctification in the Old Testament

A solid grounding in the theology of the Old Testament is indispensable for an adequate understanding of holiness in biblical and historical theology, but the subject is generally neglected, especially by English-speaking writers. In general "holiness" represents God's essential nature, rather than merely one of His several attributes or characteristics.[3] That the subject of sanctification or holiness is a major one in the Old Testament is reflected in the fact that the basic term *qadosh* appears more than eight hundred times in the canonical books of the Old Testament. The basic meaning here appears to be *separation*, that is, it implies to be set apart from the common and dedicated to the divine use. Examples of such sanctification include the sanctifying of the Sabbath day (Exodus 20:11), of the first-born (Exodus 13:2), of the mountain (Exodus 19:23), of the Nazarites (Numbers 6:5,6), of the priest (Ex. 29: 1, 9), and of a nation (Deuteronomy 7:6). The meaning of separation seems to be basic to all of the rest. There is not a single instance, among the more than eight hundred occurrences, in which the idea of separation is lacking. It has both a negative and a positive aspect: separation from the common and unclean, and a dedication to the divine.[4]

Sanctification also means recognition of the divine, or the acknowledgment of something to be uniquely separate and holy. This meaning is implicit in the command to "sanctify the Lord" (Isaiah 8:13, 5:16). For failing to sanctify or to recognize God's holiness Moses was severely disciplined (Numbers 20:12).

A third important meaning of the term is to purify or *cleanse*, said by Kittel to be the most important meaning of all.[5] In most of the Old Testament passages the idea of cleansing is a ceremonial purification. But there is also the idea of an inner, spiritual removal of sin in many passages, anticipating the New

Testament teaching of this subject (e.g., Psalms 51:7; Ezekiel 36:25-27; Isaiah 4:3, 6:7).

Thus, while most of the Old Testament usage is concerned with ceremonial defilement and its removal, there are many passages, which emphasize, in a moral or spiritual context, the idea of separation and dedication, with cleansing being clearly implied. This is a basic concept in Old Testament theology.

New Testament Usage

The basic meaning of "separation," seen in *qadosh* and its cognates, is reflected in *hagiádzo* and similar terms in the New Testament. Typical of such is 1 Corinthians 1:2—"sanctified in Christ Jesus, called to be saints."[6] The separation is twofold as is generally true of *qadosh*: negatively, from the common and the unclean, positively, unto God for His perpetual and exclusive use. Here "sanctified" is not descriptive of a high level of Christian experience, but of the initial stage of Christian conversion. Hence all Christians are separated or "sanctified" in this sense by virtue of being Christians. This basic meaning of the term may be more precisely defined as positional or imputed sanctification and is somewhat synonymous with justification, except that it has a cultic rather than forensic association.[7] It may be noted in passing that "justification" and "regeneration" are more than Pauline and Johannine terms respectively for entrance into the family of God. Justification means a change of *status* before God from guilt to guiltlessness, while regeneration is subjective and involves a change of *nature*. Justification involves a new relationship, regeneration a new life.

The second meaning of sanctification may be called *actual*, positive, or infused sanctification, and involves the impartation of God's righteous nature; it is analogous to regeneration. The Thessalonians, after conversion from pagan idolatry (1 Thessalonians 1:10), were described as "saved through sanctification of the Spirit and belief in the truth" (1 Thessalonians 2:13), a positive transformation. Likewise, 1 Peter is addressed to those "sanctified by the Spirit for obedience to Jesus Christ" (1:2). Included in the impartation of the divine nature is the hallowing that inevitably results when God invests with His own sanctity that which is devoted exclusively to Him. This appears in even the earliest New Testament literature: "God has not called us unto uncleanness but unto holiness" (1 Thessalonians 4:3-7).[8]

The third and most controverted meaning of the term is "entire sanctification" or sanctification of the inner nature consummated by the indwelling Spirit of God. The real question is, are there passages in which *hagiasmós* is linked with an advanced stage of Christian experience? Holiness is more than an antithesis to uncleanness; on the positive side it is a partaking of something of the "wholly other" purity of God. In some passages it implies the bringing of human nature, through grace, to a character of God-likeness with respect to freedom from uncleanness and sin. *Hagiasmós* admittedly refers to a "relatively mature stage of Christian experience" in two instances, but are there others as well?[9] In Romans 6:19, 22 the converts, after being told that there is no place for sin in the life of the Christian (Romans 6:1ff), are urged to yield their members "to righteousness for sanctification" in the confidence that "the return you get is sanctification and its end, eternal life." In the light of the total context in Romans, the summons to "reckon yourselves to be dead indeed unto sin" (Romans 6:11) is not an indulgence in irresponsible rhetoric but a summons to a level of holy living quite in advance of that attainable in the elementary stages of conversion.

The verb form *hagiádzw* also affords instances of this kind. Ephesians 5:26 rises above the language of cultic ritual to spiritual maturity:

> Christ loved the church and gave himself for her, That he might sanctify her, having cleansed her by the washing of water with the word, that the church might be presented to him in splendor, without spot or wrinkle or any such thing, that she might be holy and without blemish.

In 1 Thessalonians 5:23 Paul prays that "the God of peace himself sanctify you wholly," and the context makes clear that an advanced stage of sanctity, a consummation of righteousness, is intended. The same is true of 2 Timothy 2:21— "a vessel unto honor, sanctified and useful for the Master."

The noun form *hagiosúne* also affords examples of the association of these terms with Christian purity, as something separate and beyond the basic principles of Christian experience. 1 Thessalonians 3:13 calls for an establishment of "hearts unblamable in holiness." In 2 Corinthians 7:1 the words "let us cleanse ourselves from all filthiness of flesh and spirit, perfecting holiness (*epiteloúntes hagiosúne*) in the fear of God" are hardly to be identified with initiatory stages of the Christian life.

The adjectival form (*hágios*) shows a meaning more advanced than that of separation or cultic purity. In Mark 6:20, John the Baptist is described as "a righteous and holy man." 1 Peter 1:15,16, following the precedent of Leviticus 11:44, 19:2, 20:7, states that the Christian is to be holy, for God is holy; holiness then is God-likeness in one's conduct, not merely ceremonial purity. In Romans 12:1 the term is associated with a climactic call to move from the state of justification to full dedication and sanctification of every phase of life, thus becoming "holy and acceptable" unto God.

Another synonym is *hagnos*, which originally signified cultic purity but in several important passages clearly means moral blamelessness and purity of heart. Of these, 1 John 3:3 is typical—"every one who thus hopes in him purifies himself as he is pure."[10]

Hagiotes is another cognate form associated with Christian maturity. Paul, in 2 Corinthians 1:12, recalls that this ministry among them was "with simplicity and godly sincerity, not by earthly wisdom but by the grace of God"—hardly the language of a mere initiate. In Hebrews 12:10 the design of discipline is "that we may share his holiness."

When one considers the high ethical note of the New Testament writings, together with the strong moral urgency of its exhortations, the passages cited, urging a life of Christlikeness, including victory over known sin and perfect love to God, constitute a call for something over and above the initial stages of Christian living. The evidence examined appears to substantiate the conclusion that

> There is a state possible to Christians, corresponding to the ideal of their calling, in which they be described as 'unblameable in holiness'...and into which they may be brought by the grace of God in this life. Therein they shall stand hallowed through and through...every part of their being ...abiding by grace in a condition fit to bear the scrutiny of their Lord's presence without rebuke...Such is the teaching of 1 Thessalonians 3:13, 5:23.

Thus sanctification begins subjectively as faith (cf. Acts 26:18), or trustful self-abandonment to God's revealed will; and ends as love. Attitude passes into character; the soul becoming assimilated to its object, the God to whom it is consecrated. This means that Justification, which involves regeneration, is implicit Sanctification; and actual Sanctification means the subjective attitude of the justified become explicit in moral life.[11]

The Best English Translation

What are the best English equivalents of the New Testament words *hagiasmós* and *hagiádzo*? Is it true that "consecration" and "sanctification" in English usage are synonymous? In support of the aforementioned changes, it had been asserted that "consecration" means primarily man's act of dedication to God, while "sanctification" means that and also God's act in imparting sanctity to that which has been dedicated to Him. In short, both terms are used to denote "dedication," but "sanctification" has the further meaning of hallowing or cleansing, which is primarily God's work. Does the history of the English language bear this out? The words need to be traced from New Testament Greek through Ecclesiastical Latin to Medieval and Modern English. The word "consecrate" causes little difficulty: It means, "to render sacred." The term "consecratio" expresses the act of setting apart perpetually for the exclusive use of deity. It differs from "dedicatio" only in that the latter may have a secular as well as a sacred usage. None of the examples of "consecration" given in the *Oxford English Dictionary* show God doing something for man; in each case the term designates man's act of dedication to God. Typical are these instances:

1535 A.D.	Then sayde Moses; Consecrate youre handes this date unto the Lorde. —Coverdale, Exodus 32:29.
1579 A.D.	To consecrate is to hallow, or to separate to a holy use, so we grant ye bread and wine to be consecrated. —Fulke, *Hoskins*. Par. 67.
1634 A.D.	Bishop is to consecrate or dedicate the same (churches or chappels) —Coke, 3rd. *Inst*. (1644), 202.
1649 A.D.	What you have consecrated I have hallowed. —Jer. Taylor, Gt. *Exeme*. II, vii, 28.

The Oxford Dictionary gives only two examples of exceptions to the general meaning of man's act of dedication, and they are poetical metaphors:

| 1693 A.D. | So glorious a cause as consecrates each sword that's drawn for it.
—Shadwell, *Volunteers*, III, i. |
| 1887 A.D. | Whose memories seem to consecrate the soul from all ignobler championship.
—Lowell, *Democ.* 192. |

In the light of this evidence, it should afford no surprise to be told that the "consecration" of a church is something that man does.[12]

The meaning of "sanctification" is more debatable. It has two meanings as given by the Merriam-Webster Unabridged Dictionary: (a) "to make sacred or holy," in much the same meaning as "consecration"; (b) "to make free from sin; to cleanse from moral corruption and pollution, to purify." The question is whether this latter meaning is a creation of the theologians or justified by New Testament exegesis. The term is derived from two words—"sanctus" (holy) and— "ficare" (to make). The noun "sanctificium" was used by Tertullian (*Res. Carn.* 47) in referring to *hagiasmós* in Romans 6:19.[13] *The Oxford Dictionary* gives as the first meaning:

> The action of the Holy Spirit in sanctifying or making holy the believer, by the implanting within him of the Christian graces and the destruction of sinful affections. Also, the condition or process of being so sanctified.

Historical examples of this meaning include:

1645 A.D.   The renewing of our nature, according to the image of God, in righteousness and true holiness: which is begun in this life, and is called sanctification.
—Ussher, *Body Div.* (1647) 202.

1788 A.D.   By sanctification we are saved from the power and the root of sin, and restored to the image of God.
—J. Wesley, *Words* (1872) VI, 50.

1876 A.D.   Sanctification is that growth in holiness through the influence of the Holy Spirit, which must follow justification.
—J.P. Norris, *Rudim. Theol.* I, iii, 65.

The second meaning given is "the act of consecration or setting apart as holy" which is synonymous with "consecration." Illustrative of this meaning is

| 1636 A.D. | Sanctification is the setting apart of a thing for a holy or religious use, in such sort, that thereafter it may be put to no other use. —Gillispie, Eng.: *Opo. Cerem*. III, 1, 6. |

There are other special meanings cited here, most of which are used in connection with ecclesiastical rites as defined in Roman Catholic usage.

The above evidence indicates that in English usage "sanctification" has meant primarily the moral renewal of the soul while "consecration" ordinarily means dedication. This is especially true of Protestant usage.

In the light of this evidence the following conclusions seem warranted.

1) In the New Testament the terms *hagiasmós* and its cognates, supported by *hagneia* and related forms, are often found in a context expressive of the higher ranges of Christian experience, quite distinct from and subsequent to justification and regeneration.

2) The English terms used to express this teaching are commonly "sanctification" and "holiness." These terms are not normally synonymous with "consecration."

3) The view that "consecration" is normally what man dedicates to God while "sanctification" is the normal term to describe the spiritual renewal of the soul by God is supported by New Testament exegesis as well as by Protestant theological usage.

4) The alterations made in the 1952 printing of the RSVNT are justified not only by contemporary English usage but also by New Testament exegesis.

5) The New Testament consistently urges upon believers the necessity for making explicit by faith the mandate implicit in their conversion—that of a spiritual transformation into the "image of Christ." This is by Paul especially spoken of as coming by a decisive act of faith, like the faith by which they were once saved, and which tones up the entire inner life (Romans 12: 1).

"Such is the sanctification of Christian maturity, the type of life belonging to those already 'spiritual' as distinguished from 'babes in Christ' (1 Corinthians 3:1)."[14]

While the association of "sanctification" with the higher levels of Christian maturity is clearly discernible in the New Testament, the case for entire sanctification as a "second work of grace" distinct from regeneration rests not so much on explicit assertions as implicit inferences. The most specific passages are in 1 Thessalonians 3:13 and 5:23 where those clearly converted (1:10) are directed to look for an immediate renewal and consummation of their spiritual nature as a preparation for the *parousia*. In Romans 6:1, 13 the justified Christian is exhorted to make actual by faith the full deliverance over sin, which became potential when he was spiritually united with Christ. In Acts the Samaritans received the Holy Spirit as a "second work of grace," the chief significance of which was not power (Acts 8:10, 19) but purity (cf. Acts 15:9). The sum-total of these and other passages suggests, more probably than not, the conclusion that entire sanctification is a stage of Christian experience quite distinct from regeneration, not as the achievement of spiritual athletes but as a work of grace, the flowering of perfect love. In what is perhaps the latest writing of the New Testament, the author assures his Christian readers that they shall be like Christ at the *parousia*, but accompanies this hope by the present imperative to be pure in heart (1 John 3:2).

It should be kept in mind that, whatever else is involved, Christian maturity includes the following virtues:

1) It involves *Christ-likeness*. The one most mature spiritually is the one most Christ-like, whether he has experienced one or several "works of grace."

2) It involves *simplicity*. It means a sincerity, which does not perform acts of devotion ostentatiously; freedom from duplicity is meant—a "single eye."

3) It involves *aspiration* for God's best. Paul, in Philippians 3:10, voices the paradox of this position. By faith in Christ he had "arrived" after years of futile seeking within Judaism, yet at the same time he was now ardent in his pursuit of the mind of Christ.

4) It involves poverty of spirit, *humility*. The spirit of self-sufficiency is foreign to biblical holiness although characteristic of the Pharisaic type of pseudo-holiness. The parables stressing humility (the Publican: Luke 18:9) and the exhortations of mutual submission (Romans 12:3ff; Philippians 2:1-11) kept this idea prominently before the early church.

5) It involves fruitfulness. Barrenness is impossible to the healthy, growing Christian. If united with his Lord, he will be fruitful and effective. Christian perfection is not possible apart from growth, life and fruit (John 15:1).

6) It involves love and unity. Brotherly love is, according to the New Testament, the crowning

virtue, the cap-sheaf of the Christian graces, and the supreme evidence of maturity. Christian maturity, or holiness, involves more than these qualities, but it never means any less.

The Work of the Holy Spirit in Sanctification

The work of the Spirit in the renewal, cleansing, and empowering of the believer is widely recognized among evangelical churches. The work of the Spirit in removal of sin receives surprisingly little explicit treatment either in the Bible or in books concerning the Holy Spirit. Yet it is generally agreed that the agent of the Godhead in the moral purification of the soul is the Spirit of God. The Holy Spirit as the agent in sanctification receives its greatest emphasis in the literature of the Dead Sea Scrolls and in the New Testament. Before reviewing this it will be well to survey broadly the materials, which lead up to the New Testament teaching.

The Spirit of God in the Old Testament

A study of the Old Testament doctrine of the Spirit begins with a word study of the Hebrew term *ruach*, which occurs about two hundred times in the canonical Old Testament. Sometimes it is translated by "spirit" and includes man's mind or emotions as in Psalms 77:6, "I meditate and search my spirit." It also occurs as "breath" in thirty-nine of these instances. A good example of this is found in Ezekiel when the prophet, viewing the "valley of dry bones," was commanded to say, "Come, O winds, and breathe upon these slain that they may live" (Ezekiel 37:9). As a result the dry bones received spirit and live. A beautiful thought is voiced in the opening chapters of Genesis when it is said, "The Spirit of God brooded over the face of the deep," and also in the words, "God breathed into man's nostrils the breath of life..." (Genesis 1:2, 2:7). The combined meaning of "wind," "breath," and "spirit" is illustrated also at Pentecost where there is linked the energy of wind, the inspired utterance of the witnesses, and the impartation of spiritual life (Acts 2:1-35; John 3:5-8). The Old Testament teachings portray the Spirit of God as inspiring handcraft, as with Bezaleel in the tabernacle building (Exodus 31:2), giving military courage (Judas 11:29), giving authority to administrators (1 Samuel 16:13), inspiring prophecy (Ezekiel 2:2, 3), and providing cleansing from sin (Ezekiel 36:25-27). The purging of individuals by the Holy Spirit is also envisioned in the words, "Create within me a clean heart..." (Psalms 51:10).

The Inter-Testamental Period

In the Apocryphal Old Testament references to the Spirit of God are infrequent, the term "holy spirit" appearing but seven times. Accompanying this is an emphasis on the transcendence of God. The apocalypses of this period also place little stress upon the Spirit. In this literature visions and angels are the normal method of divine revelation, rather than the Spirit. In the traditions of the rabbis, which became written literature *after* the New Testament was written; the Spirit of God was represented by the Shekinah or presence of God, as in the temple. It was comparable to the *real presence* in the "host" at the altar of Catholic churches. Among evangelicals, of course, the Spirit of God is believed to indwell human personality—"Ye are the temples of the Holy Spirit" (1 Corinthians 6:19).

The Dead Sea Scrolls present a very interesting sidelight upon the development of the doctrine during this pre-Christian period. Actually, this literature appears to be somewhat of a bridge between the Old and New Testaments in its emphasis on the importance and nature of the Spirit's work as Sanctifier. There is not, however, an emphasis in the scrolls upon the Spirit as a Person. One can never be quite sure whether the term

"Holy Spirit," in this Qumran literature, refers to the Spirit of God or to the human spirit in which God is welcomed. In one remarkable passage in the *Manual of Discipline* the cleansing work of the Holy Spirit is stressed:

> God will purge all the acts of men in the crucible of his truth and refine for himself all the fabric of man, destroying every spirit of perversity from within his flesh and cleansing him by the Holy Spirit from all the effects of wickedness. Like waters of purification he will sprinkle upon him the Spirit of Truth, to cleanse him of all the abominations of falsehood and all of the pollution through the spirit of filth to the end that being made upright man may have the understanding of transcendental knowledge and of the Lord of the sons of heaven and that being made blameless in their ways they may be endued with an inner vision.[15]

The inner cleansing then comes by the Holy Spirit, also described as the "Spirit of Truth." The "waters of purification" remind one of baptism, of Ezekiel's words in his prophecy (36:26), likewise the prophecy of Joel. Twenty places in the Qumran literature the term "Holy Spirit" occurs. The need for the Spirit of God in cleansing of the nature is emphasized as much as in the Old Testament and much more so than either the Apocrypha or of the rabbinic writings. Nowhere, except in Acts 15:9, is the cleansing from sin so explicitly associated with the Holy Spirit.

The New Testament

From the standpoint of the doctrine of the Spirit the New Testament reflects a mighty upsurge, an emphasis upon God at work with His people. The word "spirit," which in all its varied meanings appears in the Hebrew Old Testament 203 times, occurs 386 times in the much shorter New Testament. The word "holy" is associated with "Spirit" eighty-eight times in the New Testament as compared with three times in the Old. This supports Peter's declaration that Joel's prophesy was actually fulfilled in the New Testament times and is reflected in the literature that the Christians considered uniquely inspired.

The *work* of the Spirit in the New Testament is a rich study. It includes that of revealing Christ to the disciples as we learn from John 15:26 and 16:14: "He shall take the things of mine and show them unto you." Also, the work of the Spirit is that of *revealing* sin to the unbeliever, as we learn in John 16:8: "He shall reprove the world of sin, and of righteousness, and of judgment." In addition, the work of the Spirit is that of *revealing truth* to the future believer: "When he, the Spirit of Truth, is come, he will lead you into all truth" (John 16: 13). A major work of the Spirit in the New Testament is that of inspiring believers to witness) as we learn from Acts 1:8: "When the Holy Spirit is come upon you, you shall be my witnesses." Almost equally important was the work of the Spirit in inspiring those under persecution in their *defense*. Jesus had told them to take no thought beforehand what to say because the Spirit would teach them (Mark 13:11). Many instances show how this was actually fulfilled (e.g, Acts 4:8). Finally, the work of the Spirit was that of *purifying* hearts of believers, as we learn in Acts 15:9 where Peter sums up both his experience at Pentecost and the experience of Cornelius by saying, "Their hearts were purified by faith." In summary, the New Testament presents the Holy Spirit as *illuminating*, giving *power* to witness, affording *courage* under persecution, and *cleansing* the heart from sin.

The Baptism of the Holy Spirit

Dispensational viewpoint. Because of the misunderstanding over this issue, it seems well to devote careful attention to an exposition of the New Testament doctrine of the Baptism of the Holy Spirit. Two major views are those held by the Reformed tradition and those of the Arminian-Wesleyan tradition. Among those holding the Reformed view are representatives of the so-called Dispensational viewpoint. According to this view, which is zealously set forth by John Walvoord and Merrill Unger of Dallas Theological Seminary, as well as Arno C. Gaebelein and the late Dr. E. Y. Mullins of Southern Baptist Seminary, there is only one dispensational, historic Pentecost and baptism of the Holy Spirit. This was given at a certain time in God's plan to the believers as a whole, and since this is an accomplished historical fact, the believer needs only to recognize it. Consequently, when a person believes on Christ and is saved, he is invariably baptized with the Holy Spirit. In words of Unger, "The regenerating work of the Holy Spirit never occurs apart from his simultaneous baptizing, indwelling, in sealing,... simultaneously, and eternally in the believer the moment he believes."[16] According to this view the whole matter is to be interpreted in the light of 1 Corinthians 12:13, "For by one Spirit we were all baptized into one body—Jews or Greeks, slaves or free—and all were made to drink of one Spirit." This baptism is regarded as positional rather than personal and experiential. The emphasis is upon the objective rather than the subjective factor. In support of this, Mullins urges that there is only one such baptism—that described in Acts 2, and that the outpouring of the Spirit in the eighth, tenth, and nineteenth chapters of Acts were "not baptisms of the Spirit in the strict sense," but instances of "the reception by believers of the Spirit already bestowed at Pentecost."[17] As for the bestowal upon Cornelius in Acts 10, it was only a completion of the one baptism at

Pentecost. In other words, advocates of this point of view would hold that the baptism of the Holy Spirit occurred only once in history at Pentecost, but it was in three or four installments. It is to be regarded as one historic event and not to be repeated in the life of any individual believer since then except at conversion. They note that there is no command to be baptized with the spirit, though there is a command to be filled with the Spirit. In other words, when you become a Christian you are then baptized with the Holy Spirit; this marks the initial phase of salvation.

Evangelical Reformed view. A modification of this view sees a distinction between the sealing of the Spirit at conversion and the baptism or filling of the Spirit later. Some of these in the Reformed tradition are Calvinists who have been awakened by the Spirit and have walked in His light. Consequently they come close to believing in a "second crisis experience." Many of them say that this second crisis experience is involved with a filling of the Spirit but it does not lead to entire cleansing from sin. The only difference between them and those in the Wesleyan tradition would be at the factor of the deliverance from all sin. C. R. Erdman states that:

> It is undoubtedly true that there are those to whom the experience of being filled with the Spirit of Christ has come to a sudden and epochal crisis. After long years of fruitlessness and failure some secret sin has been abandoned, some long neglected tasks undertaken, some definite surrender to Christ has been made, there is resulted a power and service never before experienced, a love for others never before known.[18]

In a similar manner, F. B. Meyer writes:

> Certainly the Holy Spirit has been at work within you, else you were none of Christ's. But there is an experience altogether beyond and above this initial step by which the Holy Spirit first reveals sin and Christ, and it is for lack of this that your testimony is so inoperative and your lives so destitute of fire.[19]

Meyer goes on to note the difference between having the Holy Spirit and being filled with the Spirit. He adds:

> How many Christians complain of the uprising of their old depraved nature, which so rapidly responds to suggestions of the tempter betraying the continued presence in the heart of that self-principle which is the cause of all the evil and misery of the world. This is largely because there has been no deep experience of the filling of the Holy Spirit.[20]

Thomas Waugh comes even closer to the Arminian-Wesleyan position. He notes that the disciples illustrate that the results before and after Pentecost indicate that "The first effect of this baptism of the Spirit of fire is to destroy sin in the soul."[21] He adds that this does not come because of our efforts to cleanse ourselves but by our making room for the incoming Holy Spirit. These statements illustrate what happens when those in the Reformed tradition respond to all the light revealed in the New Testament.

Wesleyan Position. As one looks at the Arminian-Wesleyan view of the baptism of the Holy Spirit he is surprised at the relative scarcity of materials dealing with the connection between entire sanctification, perfect love, and the baptism of the Holy Spirit, points at which one would expect to find clear explication. It would seem that the preachers give far more attention to it than the writers in the same tradition. John Fletcher actually writes of baptism of the Spirit at conversion.

The advocate of the Arminian-Wesleyan view would affirm, first, that the baptism of the Holy Spirit is distinct from water baptism, as seen in Matthew 3:11, Mark 1:8, Luke 3:16, John 1:33, and Acts 1:5. It is significant that Jesus baptized with water (John 3:22,26, 4:1,2), as well as with the Holy Spirit. It would seem, therefore, that if the baptism of the Holy Spirit is to be regarded as a once-for-all and hence unrepeatable event, then surely the baptism of John should be likewise so regarded. However, if water baptism is to be perpetuated, then the baptism of the Spirit should also be perpetuated as something distinct from water baptism. If it were argued that the baptism of the Spirit as a commanded experience is not emphasized in the Epistles, it may be added that neither is the command to be baptized given prominence there. Contrary to the Dispensationalist view, the baptism of the Spirit indicated in 1 Corinthians 12:13 refers to that which occurred at the initial water baptism and places stress upon the resulting unity. It is the Spirit that does the baptizing rather than Jesus baptizing in the Spirit, and the stress there is not on the baptism but upon the unity, which results from one's being incorporated into the spiritual body of Christ. This unity is in line with that envisioned in Ephesians 4:4, 5.

The Promise of the Father

According to the Gospels, the believers in Jesus possessed the gift of the Spirit (cf. Luke 11:13), but lived in anticipation of His historic outpouring at Pentecost. Caution is needed here lest a chronological sequence caused by the gradual unfolding of God's purpose in fulfillment of prophecy be construed as the normal pattern of Christians today. With Jesus' departure imminent, the need for the indwelling energy and wisdom of the Spirit became more urgent. Accordingly, in Luke, John, and Acts the disciples are prepared both for the Master's leaving and for the Holy Spirit's coming in a climactic manner. In Luke 11:13 the disciples were taught to ask for the gift of the Spirit; in Luke 24:49 Jesus stated that He would send the Holy Spirit soon; in Acts they were exhorted to "wait for the promise of the Father" (Acts 1:4). That this promised gift is identical with the baptism of the Holy Spirit is evident from Acts 1:5: "Ye shall be baptized with the Holy Spirit not many days hence." Its fulfillment is recorded in the words of Peter: "Having received of the Father the promise of the Holy Spirit he hath poured forth this" (Acts 2:33).

The Spirit comes to *every believer at conversion*, creating within him a new heart, revealing Christ as Savior, sealing him unto the day of redemption and witnessing to his adoption into the family of God. Henceforth, as he "walks in the light" he is a participant in the "Spirit bearing community" (the *Koinonia*). Subsequent to this he needs to be "sanctified in truth," "filled with the Spirit," and "endued with power from on high." The disciples had received the Holy Spirit when Jesus breathed upon them after the resurrection (John 20:22), but they still needed the baptizing, cleansing, and empowering of the Spirit. Peter, in reviewing the outpouring of the Spirit at Pentecost, and subsequently at the home of Cornelius, summed it up as "cleansing our hearts by faith" (Acts 15:9). This was more than inclusion into the Christian community; more than a rite of initiation; it was the purification enjoined in Romans 6 and elsewhere in the Epistles. As E. Stanley Jones has expressed it: in regeneration we have the Spirit; in entire sanctification the Spirit has us. It involves not only pardon for known sins but in Jones' words, a "cleansing of the sub-conscious."

Questions Often Needing Clarification

Does the Holy Spirit come to believers at conversion or only at a second crisis experience? The Scripture shows clearly that He comes at conversion. Actually, He comes even before that to show the sinner his need (John 16:8; Acts 2:37). The coming of the Spirit is linked with water baptism at conversion, as implied in John 3:5; Acts 2:38; Titus 1; Corinthians 12:13. The sealing of the Spirit appears to be also at conversion (Ephesians 1:14, 4:30; 2 Corinthians 1:21, 22). In the language of John 14:17, He is *with* the disciples from conversion but not in them until after Pentecost.

Perhaps it would be correct to say that in Johannine writings the work of the Spirit as *teacher* is stressed. In the Synoptics and Acts, the *power* of the Spirit is stressed, while Paul's epistles emphasize the *purifying* work of the Spirit. The Corinthians were concerned with the charismatic aspect of the Spirit's work in His numerous gifts. The apostle was even more concerned with the ethical effects and with holy living, whence he said, "If you are in the Spirit, by the Spirit also let us walk" (Galatians 5:25). Paul would say that the spiritual man is judged not by his abundance of gifts but by his holy living (1 Corinthians 13). It is of great importance to keep these three emphases in perspective— the work of the Spirit in *illuminating, empowering* and *purifying*. We certainly are in line with Paul's great concern when we remember that the graces of the Spirit are more important than the gifts of the Spirit, and that the most spiritual person is the one who is most Christ-like; as Schliermacher expressed it: "The graces of the Spirit are the virtues of Christ." Certainly the church has no need greater than that of being entirely sanctified and filled with the Holy Spirit. Such was the case in the first century as evidenced by the Acts of the Apostles. We need to be Spirit-filled today to have an effective witness to the world. We need also to be Spirit-filled to have a witness to those church groups that have largely lost their message and mission. One church leader, after comparing the progress of the newer sects with the "stagnation" of the older denominations, remarked: "We need more spizerinctum." A Spirit-filled church would be the answer to his dilemma.

How can one be filled with the Spirit? First by *confession* of spiritual need: "Blessed are the poor in spirit." A confession by a child of God that he needs the filling and cleansing power of the Spirit is as essential as the sinner confessing his guilt. Second, *petition* is essential: "How much more will your Heavenly Father give the Holy Spirit to those who ask him?" Third, *consecration*: "To the extent that we consecrate the Spirit sanctifies." The sinner surrenders; the child of God can dedicate his will, his all, himself. Fourth, *faith* is the avenue of every blessing. "Faithful is he who calls you, who also will do it."

Notes

---

[1] H. W. Perkins, *The Doctrine of Christian or Evangelical Perfection* (London: Epworth Press, 1927), *passim*.

[2] C. T. Craig, "The Paradox of Holiness," *Interpretation* (April, 1952), pp. 152ff.

[3] Ragnor Asting, *Die Heiligkeit im Urchristentum* (Gottingen: Vandenhoeck & Ruprecht, 1930), p. 17.

[4] G. A. Turner, *The More Excellent Way* (Winona Lake, Ind.: Light and Life Press, 1952), pp. 23ff.

[5] R. Kittel, "Holiness," Schaff-Herzog, *Encyclopedia of Religious Knowledge*, V. 317.

[6] Other examples of this usage: Romans 1:7; 1 Corinthians 1:30; 1 Corinthians 6:11.

[7] See also Craig, *op. cit.,* pp. 151f.

[8] Other examples of this meaning are: Matt. 6:9; Acts 20:32; 26:18; 1 Corinthians 7:14; 1 Timothy 4:5; Hebrew 2:22; 9:13; 10:10, 29.

[9] 1 Timothy 2:15 and Hebrews 12:14. See Craig, *op. cit.,* p. 153.

[10] See also Jas. 4:8; I Tim. 4:12; 5:2 and Procksch in G. Kittell, *Theologishes Wörterbuch zum New Testament*, I (1936-), 123f.

[11] J. V. Bartlet, "Sanctification," in Hastings' *Dictionary of the Bible*, IV, 393f.

[12] Cf. Craig, *op. cit.,* p. 149.

[13] Andrews, *Latin-English Lexicon* (New York: Harpers, 1950). Tr. "holiness" by Holmes, *The Ante-Nicene Fathers* (New York: Scribners, 1899), III, 580.

[14] Bartlet, *op. cit.,* p. 393.

[15] T. H. Gaster, *The Dead Sea Scriptures* (Garden City, New York: Doubleday, 1956), p. 45.

[16] M. F. Unger, "The Baptism with the Holy Spirit," *BIBLIOTHECA SACRA*, April-Sept. (1944), V. 101, pp. 232ff.

[17] E. Y. Mullins, "Baptism of the Holy Spirit," *I. S. B. E.*, I, 401.

[18] C. R. Erdman, *The Spirit of Christ* (New York: Richard R. Smith, 1929), p. 44.

[19] F. B. Meyer, "The Filling of the Holy Spirit," in T. Waugh, Ed., *The Power of Pentecost* (Chicago: The Bible Institute Colportage Association, N. d.), p. 116.

[20] *Ibid.,* p. 120.

[21] *Ibid.,* p. 59.

www.ingramcontent.com/pod-product-compliance
Lightning Source LLC
Chambersburg PA
CBHW061740020426
42331CB00006B/1310